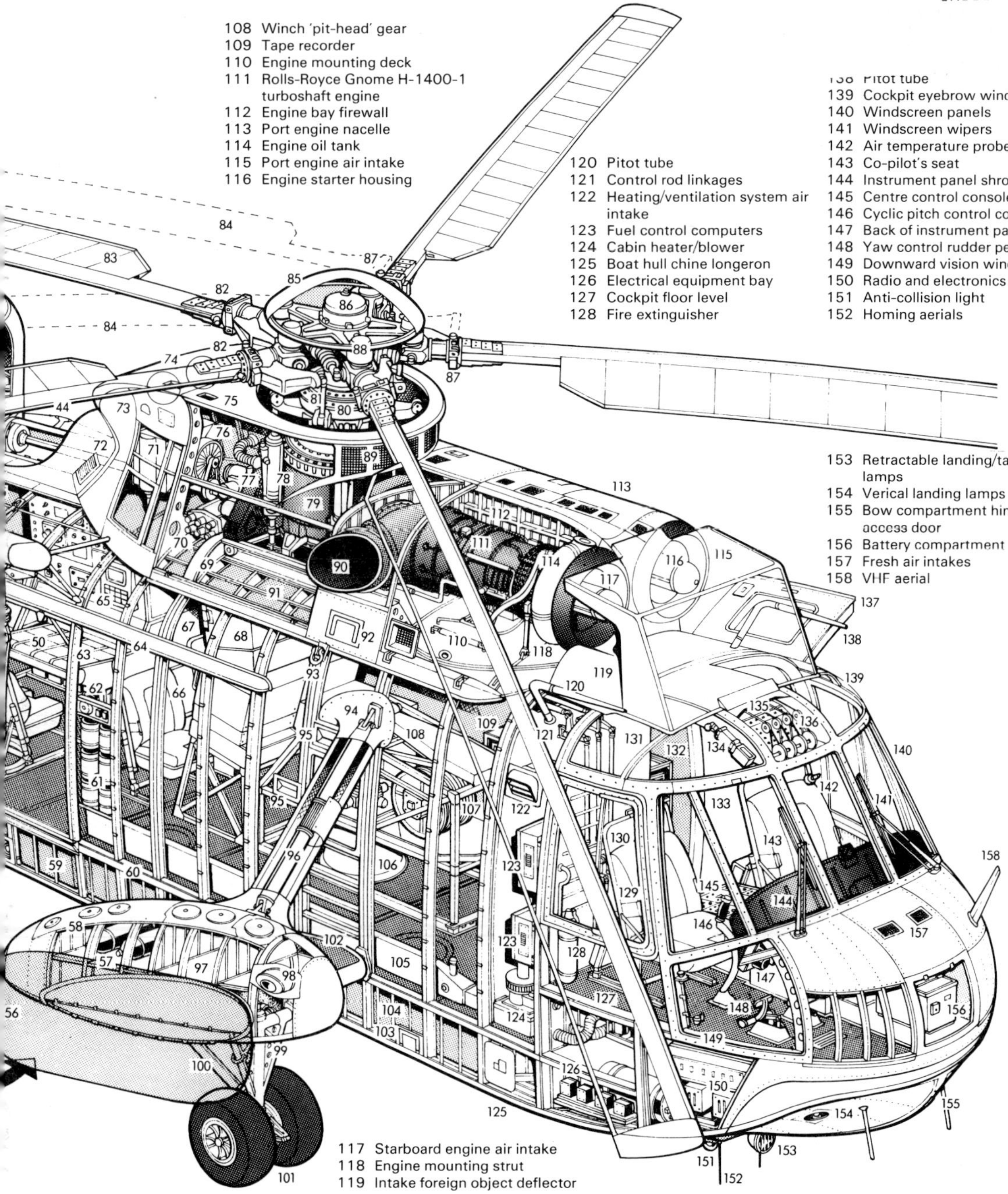

108 Winch 'pit-head' gear
109 Tape recorder
110 Engine mounting deck
111 Rolls-Royce Gnome H-1400-1 turboshaft engine
112 Engine bay firewall
113 Port engine nacelle
114 Engine oil tank
115 Port engine air intake
116 Engine starter housing

117 Starboard engine air intake
118 Engine mounting strut
119 Intake foreign object deflector

120 Pitot tube
121 Control rod linkages
122 Heating/ventilation system air intake
123 Fuel control computers
124 Cabin heater/blower
125 Boat hull chine longeron
126 Electrical equipment bay
127 Cockpit floor level
128 Fire extinguisher

138 Pitot tube
139 Cockpit eyebrow windows
140 Windscreen panels
141 Windscreen wipers
142 Air temperature probe
143 Co-pilot's seat
144 Instrument panel shroud
145 Centre control console
146 Cyclic pitch control column
147 Back of instrument panel
148 Yaw control rudder pedals
149 Downward vision window
150 Radio and electronics equipment
151 Anti-collision light
152 Homing aerials

153 Retractable landing/taxying lamps
154 Verical landing lamps
155 Bow compartment hinged access door
156 Battery compartment
157 Fresh air intakes
158 VHF aerial

592
CU
ROYAL N

Modern Combat Aircraft 18

Westland SEA KING

John Chartres

LONDON
IAN ALLAN LTD

Acknowledgements

Any lay author dealing with such a complex subject as this obviously has to pick the brains of many others. This list of acknowledgements and thanks is therefore a long one. Properly it should be even longer, but I wish to name the following for their special help: Peter Batten of Westland PLC; Bob Bryanton formerly of Rolls-Royce; Horace Field of Sikorskys; Gordon Swanborough, Editor of *Air International*, especially for permission to draw on information from two articles, 'Superior Sub-Hunter' and 'Omnifarious Sea King'; the editor of *Defence* for access to information about the latest Sikorsky projects; my ever-generous professional colleague and fellow helicopter enthusiast, James D. Ferguson of Aberdeen; fellow authors Lt-Cdr James Milne (*Flashing Blades Over the Sea*) and Geoffrey Underwood (*Our Falklands War*) and their publisher, Michael Critchley of Maritime Books.

Among the many friends I have made in the Fleet Air Arm I must especially thank Cdrs Victor Sirett and Paul Madge; Lt-Cdrs David Beswick, Robin Everall and Brian Morgan; Lts Alan Brooks (No 819 Squadron) and Chris Wood (No 814 Squadron); 2nd Officer Sue Eagles WRNS and Fleet CPO Stephen Hobden.

Within the RAF 'Sea King World' I would like to thank Wg Cdr Ivan Hughes and his Adjutant in the SAR Wing, Flt Lt David Cardus; Flt Lt Jeremy English (formerly Lt RN) as well as many old friends from the days of the research into my earlier book, *Helicopter Rescue*.

To all the others unnamed, who build, fly or maintain Sea Kings, and who obviously share my feeling of enthusiasm for them, I would also like to say 'thank-you', not only for their readiness to give me information and advice but for the pleasure of their company, which has made the work entirely enjoyable.

John Chartres
Hale, Cheshire

First published 1984

ISBN 0 7110 1394 2

Published by Ian Allan Ltd, Shepperton, Surrey; and printed by Ian Allan Printing Ltd at their works at Coombelands in Runnymede, England.

Contents

Roots

Above: It is difficult for any designer to make a helicopter look aesthetically beautiful but some can at least be made to look purposeful, and therefore 'look right'. A Mk 1 Sea King landing on HMS *Blake* and 'looking right'. *Westland*

Below: An HAR Mk 3 Sea King of No 202 Squadron RAF on dawn readiness at Lossiemouth. *Cpl Mike Hume/RAF*

During one of the scores of conversations with airmen which have enlivened the research into this book, a naval aviator of great renown and experience said:

'Whatever you write about the Sea King now, I would hazard a guess that an air historian of the future will bracket it with the dear old Dakota — in that it *looked* right from the start, it *felt* right, it *was* right and it was probably going to go on flying for ever.'

At the time of writing this book the Sea King design concept was 26 years old. Sea Kings of various varieties, perhaps more accurately dubbed 'members of the Sikorsky S-61 family' had been flying for 24 years and all informed speculation suggested some of them would go on doing so into the 21st century. This book is primarily about the British-built Westland Sea King, the first production version of which, sold to the Royal Navy, rolled out of a hangar at Yeovil in August 1969, rather a long time distant from the first flight of the Sikorsky S-61 (company designation) of HSS-2 (United States Navy early designation) on 11 March 1959.

There were many reasons for this time gap, some, but by no means all, attributable to dilatoriness on the part of governments of the day and the lack of an effective all-British helicopter industry. A great deal had to be proved before the S-61/Sea King design was adopted in Britain as the best answer to the ever-growing threat from 'opposition' submarines.

A reasonable understanding of the importance of the aircraft to this nation requires a fairly long backward look into the evolution of the helicopter as a practical form of flying machine, and particularly into the far-sightedness of certain Lords of the Admiralty (a breed not always properly credited with such a quality) and that of Fleet Air Arm (FAA) officers of widely varying ranks. Indeed the real history of the Sea King or the S-61 'family' design, which has impinged in no small way on the conduct of two wars (the Americans' long dreary one in Vietnam and our short sharp one in the Falklands), and which has had a direct bearing on the continuation of the lives of thousands of servicemen and civilians, could be taken back to 13 May 1940 when Igor Sikorsky made the first helicopter fly properly (outside Nazi Germany).

Left: What it is all about. A Mk 1 Sea King from HMS *Tiger* extracting its sonar 'body'. *Westland*

Below: When it all really started. Igor Sikorsky lifts his first VS-300 a few inches off the ground on 14 September 1939.

The Early Helicopters

The Sikorsky VS300 helicopter was not really a new invention. It was the result of an 'infinite capacity for taking pains' — the generally accepted definition of a genius — on the part of its designer to put together the results of previous experiments and failures and make the whole work.

The next stage in the whole saga leading up to the evolution of the Sea King was the design and production of some remarkable little rotary wing aircraft known in US parlance as R-4s, in British and especially Royal Navy language as Hoverflies. (Somebody did want to call them 'Gadflies' at one stage, just as somebody originally wanted to call the Sea King the Sea Dragon.) It has come as something of a surprise to many in recent years that Allied helicopters were in action during World War 2, R-4s of the USAAF rescuing American aircrews and British soldiers in the Burma theatre, and RN-owned aircraft of the same type proving that they could fly on and off a ship during the sailing of an Atlantic convoy. (Perhaps fortunately for all, the leaders of the German nation did not realise what a prize they had in their advanced helicopter designs of the 1940s, and either chose not to exploit them or were prevented from doing so by the sheer necessity of having to concentrate their aircraft industry upon fighters and bombers.) During the course of all this development very close links indeed had been established between the British armed forces and their American counterparts on the general development of rotary winged aircraft. Inevitably these links drew the British to the headquarters of the Sikorsky Aircraft Corporation at Stratford, Connecticut and a little later to the US Coastguard training station at Floyd Bennett Field, New York.

In the sort of perverse manner which seems to characterise many advances made by the British nation it was a senior naval officer, Capt Caspar John, then British Director of Naval Development & Production and later Admiral of the Fleet Sir Caspar John, who sent an RAF officer, Wg Cdr Reginald Brie, over to the States in 1941 to try to interest the American forces in the potential of the British-built Cierva Autogiroes ('free-wheeling' rotary-wing aircraft) in a future anti-submarine role. While there Wg Cdr Brie saw demonstrations of both the VS300 and the R-4 and instantly appreciating the different between the autogyro (Auto*giro* if built under Cierva patent) and the true helicopter with power delivered directly to its main rotor blades, signalled back to his masters his assessment of the 'full import of a great event'. Alongside Wg Cdr Brie at these events was Cdr J H. Millar RN, and both saw the enormous potential for their respective services of a low-flying, slow-flying aircraft which could actually stand still in the air, and even go backwards. Cdr Millar especially noted that it was a type of aircraft which could land on and take off from even small ships at sea, and could become the best weapon available against any surface Navy's real enemy — the submarine.

The RN's interest in the American helicopter developments continued through the 1940s even though the aircraft of that era fell far short of its long-term dreams of an airborne 'hunter-killer' which could at last match the submarine, which had altered all naval strategy and tactics from the early days of World War 1. At this stage senior officers of the RAF were only taking a passing interest in this ugly form of flying machine, although some of the most far-sighted pilots, many of them holding junior rank, saw its potential. So did a number of Army officers, but it was the RN which had its sights clear on the future of the helicopter, and it was its view, and that of its opposite number on the other side of the Atlantic, which led to the evolution of the Sea King.

The first helicopter training course for British pilots began in March 1944 at Floyd Bennett Field with six RN students, two RAF and one from the British Army — which even at that stage was dreaming of the formation of an Army Air Corps, eventually to be realised via the helicopter. A total of 240 Sikorsky R-4Bs (Hoverflies) was ordered by the RN in the late 1940s. In fact only 45 were delivered due to the conclusion of World War 2. The majority of the R-4s reaching this side of the Atlantic went to the FAA for intensive examination and evaluation. A few went to the RAF for rather more desultory experiments.

The future of the helicopter as a naval weapon was proved in a typically spectactular manner in September 1946 when a Lt Alan Bristow RN landed an R-4 on board HMS *Helmsdale*, a 'River' class frigate, at the start of a series of trials designed to prove that the helicopter could be an anti-submarine (AS) weapon. The name of the lieutenant concerned is now fairly well known in the commercial helicopter world.

The other important event in the evolution of naval helicopters and therefore that of the Sea King was the voyage of the British merchantman *Daghestan*, as part of a 50-ship convoy across the Atlantic in 1944 with two R-4s on board. The flight trials crew constituted one RN pilot, two RAF pilots and one from the US Coastguard Service. It was a rough crossing

Below: The RN assessed the value of the helicopter rather earlier than the other two British armed forces. Lt Ken Reed RN demonstrated that helicopters would have a future in the Navy by landing an R-4 on HMS *Vanguard* in 1947 in the presence of the Royal Family who were on their way to South Africa. *RN*

Right: The much-desired hunter-killer. A Mk 2 Sea King launching the first of its weapon-load of homing torpedoes. *RN*

Below: The Royal Navy's line-up of helicopters in the 1950s. From top to bottom: an S-51 — later to become the Dragonfly, an 'R-6' — which was a bit of an interim failure — and a faithful R-4 Hoverfly being piloted, as was the style of the time, by a naval officer wearing his peaked uniform cap, and nothing else in the way of survival gear. *RN*

Left: The first combat use the RN identified for the helicopter was the rescue of downed aircrew. Because its Dragonflies could only accommodate one payload a pilot and one aircrewman the 'Sproule Net' was devised by a most inventive naval officer of that name. This picture was taken on an exercise/demonstration, but many FAA crews were in fact plucked from the sea to fly again another day by this device.

and the little R-4s constituted no threat to any lurking U-boat packs but at least the USCG pilot managed a take-off and landing in mid-Atlantic, thus proving that the helicopter was eventually going to be a naval weapon of war.

The RN was, however, going to wait a long time before it had in its hands a fully effective airborne submarine hunter-killer in the form of the Sea King. The first and most obvious problem which had to be overcome in turning the helicopter into an effective anti-submarine weapon was the simple and basic one of 'payload'. Remarkably efficient though they were for their day, the R-4 Hoverflies could just about manage the pilot and one passenger (loaded weight 2,530lb). The next helicopter type off the Sikorsky line, the S-51 later built under licence by Westlands as the Dragonfly, could manage a two-man crew plus two or more passengers according to fuel state and general conditions. Helicopter operations within the RN in the latter days of World War 2 and into the 1950s tended therefore to be limited to such mundane tasks as practising torpedo tracking, photography, radar alignment, VIP ferrying and a certain amount of 'looking-over-the-horizon' reconnaissance.

Nevertheless the Navy was gaining experience and expertise and, importantly, building up a rotary-wing organisation. The first all-helicopter squadron outside the US, No 705 Naval Air Squadron (NAS), was formed in 1947. *Most* importantly, plans were being laid for the future by some very senior officers who perhaps even then foresaw the end of the conventional fixed-wing aircraft carrier in a nation which simply would not be able to afford such devices in the financial and strategic conditions of the 1980s. They saw their FAA's future lying under the wings (rotary or fixed) of aircraft which could fly low and slow and which above all could both hunt *and kill* submarines.

The deliveries of the Westland-built Dragonflies from June 1950 marked the next stage of progress. At least these aircraft with a loaded weight of 5,500lb and equipped with a winch (or hoist in US terms) offered the RN its first genuine combat helicopters which could be used effectively in the *combat* role of Search & Rescue. The rescue capability of the helicopter was of particular importance to the FAA because of the high risk of deck landings and take-offs and the number of aircraft which went over the side of the earlier fixed-wing carriers. (There is still among the general public something of a misconception about the role of RN and RAF rescue helicopters, particularly those based on shore in the UK. They have always been provided primarily for the military task of rescuing servicemen, especially aircrews, and even if 90% of their 'business' these days involves helping civilians and some of the funding comes from outside the Defence Vote they are really a bonus to the public at large.) The Dragonflies provided a marked improvement on the capabilities of the Walrus and Sea Otter amphibians which had themselves superseded the attendant destroyers of the 1930s.

The morale effect upon all sailors, soldiers and airmen of a helicopter rescue service has been proved time and again in all the so-called minor wars in which Britain and the US have been involved from the Malayan Emergency and Korea through to the Falklands. As later chapters will tell the Sea Kings have emerged as rescue vehicles par excellence, never more so than in the last-named conflict in which scores of servicemen lived to fight another day because of them. Rescue might be classed as very much a part of the aircraft's combat capability.

The next most important chronological event in the sequence leading up to the Sea King took place on 10 November 1949 in the USA when an aircraft designated the Sikorsky S-55 first flew. With a payload of up to eight armed troops or equivalent and a range of up to 300 miles this aircraft attracted immediate attention among all three armed forces on both sides of the Atlantic and indeed throughout the Western world. Staying in production for more than 10 years and in service for more than 25, the S-55 'family', like most

Above: The Royal Navy proved the value of the helicopter as a rescue vehicle beyond all possible doubt during the Dutch floods disaster of 1953. A Dragonfly of No 705 Naval Air Squadron (NAS) over the disaster area — one of nine aircraft which lifted 800 people to safety. *Westland*

Right: An S-55 of No 848 NAS on operations from a wettish airstrip in Borneo during the 'confrontation war' of the 1960s. *RN*

Sikorsky designed helicopters, flew under a bewildering assortment of designations and marks; it was built under licence by Westlands in Britain, Mitsubishi in Japan and SNCA du Sud-Est in France, but was and is of course best known to the British public as the Whirlwind. For the British and the US navies its most important attribute, and the one which marked the next step towards the evolution of the Sea King, was that the payload made the carrying of 'dunking sonar' equipment and a crew to operate it a practical proposition. Between 1952 and 1953 the RN obtained delivery of 27 S-55s, 12 being given the designation of HAR (Helicopter Air Rescue) Mk 21, 15 under the designation HAS (Helicopter Anti-Submarine) Mk 22.

The HAS designation was of deep significance because the art of warfare between surface ship hunter-killers and hunted submarines was already turning in favour of the latter with the evasive capability provided by the German-invented schnorkel and was about to turn even further that way with the arrival on scene of the 'nuclears' which while submerged could out-distance the fastest frigate. In both navies the first step had arrived on a long ladder climb towards the 'frigate of the future' — the hunter-killer helicopter — but with a good many years to go before the dream was realised in the form of the Sea King.

The first of the HAS 22s with their crews were formed into No 706 NAS, the aircraft being fitted with the American AN-AQS4 short range 'active sonar'. The Squadron was commissioned at Lee-on-Solent in September 1953 and then sent to Royal Naval Air Station Eglinton, near Londonderry, Northern Ireland where there were good facilities to exercise with submarines. Six months later No 706 NAS was temporarily disbanded, to reappear later with a significant role to play in the development of the Sea King and No 845 Squadron formed in its place. (In the FAA, experimental, training and other 'second line' squadrons carry the figure 7 as the first digit, front-line squadrons the figure 8.)

The RN was now in the helicopter versus submarine business. The HAS22s were shortly to be built under licence by Westlands under the designation HAS Mk 7 and another step up the ladder towards the airborne frigate had been taken.

This is probably an appropriate point at which to endeavour to explain the principles of sonar, since they are so closely interwoven with the eventual development of the Sea King. I am grateful to Lt-Cdr James Milne RN, a FAA Observer of vast experience, now a member of the Department of Naval Air Warfare staff, and author of *Flashing Blades over the Sea*, for much of the following.

There are two fundamental types of sonar equipment used in the detection of submarines — active, often referred to in the aviation world as 'dipping' or 'dunking'; and passive, sometimes referred to as 'throwaway'. Until fairly recent years the helicopter has been principally concerned with the former variety.

Active Sonar

The basic principle of active sonar, (known as Asdic during World War 2 Battle of the Atlantic) is that of the echo. Sound is reflected from a solid mass such as the side of a mountain if one shouts in a canyon, and returns to the ears of the shouter after a time interval which can be measured.

Sound at normal human frequency range does not travel through water, so electrically generated higher frequencies are used in the AS warfare art from a transducer (later to be referred to as the sonar buoy or body) which is lowered into the sea, the submarine's natural hiding place. On meeting a solid body in the water some of the sound will be returned to the transducer, which is acting as both transmitter and receiver.

The transducer is designed so that the outgoing sound can by transmitted in different patterns from pencil-beam narrowness to quite wide arcs. To obtain a bearing on the reflecting object — hopefully the enemy submarine — the transducer rotates about its cable and is linked to the helicopter's compass system, displaying the bearing in a variety of ways to the helicopter Observer.

There are however complications, because in sea water echoes can be produced by a wide variety of objects and by water conditions such as salinity variations and temperature layers. Among the objects producing echoes can be shoals of simple fish like mackerel, wrecks on the seabed, the wakes of ships (including submarines making rapid turns and producing 'knuckles' of foam) and in particular the larger sea mammals, most especially the whales, many of which it was feared met untimely ends during the Falklands conflict at the hands of torpedoes launched by ASW Sea Kings of the RN. Everyone was sad about this but it could not have been avoided.

All these factors demand the utmost sophistication in the sonar equipment itself, the methods of using it, and above all the personal skill of the operators. This skill can only be borne out of experience and training. Whatever the comparative standards of its equipment vis-a-vis that in US aircraft and in those of the 'opposition', officers of the FAA are confident that their back-room crews are the best in the world when it comes to distinguishing between the note of a 'ping' from a submarine and that from a shoal of mackerel. Distinguishing the ping of a submarine from that of a whale is rather more difficult and is perhaps the ultimate challenge to a device called the Ear, Human, Mk 1, which remains the most important part of the equipment of a Mk 5 Sea King, costing several millions of pounds sterling, and filled with the best available electronics in the Western World. The possessors of this device are called Observers and Naval Aircrewmen and more about them will be recorded later.

The use of active sonar by surface ships dates back of course to the Battle of the Atlantic but has always been limited in its effectiveness because the transducer has usually had to be operated at a fixed depth below the surface of the sea, or below the ship's hull. Variable Depth Sonar (VDS) has been developed however, and used with variable success.

The helicopter excels first and foremost because it can *exploit* water conditions and use the best depths suited to the obtaining of maximum range from its sonar buoy. In the cat-and-mouse game between hunter and hunted the helicopter has the added advantage of speed (even its modest, in aviation terms, 100kts or so in level flight) over that of the fastest submerged nuclear vessel. It also has the ability to move about in a manner unpredictable to the wiliest enemy submarine commander.

There is a special requirement for effective dunking sonar operations. The buoy, and therefore its cable, should be as near as possible to the vertical. This requirement produced problems at the early stages of the development of the art, but curiously the solutions to them proved to be two-fold — the sonar cable itself turned out to be a vital constituent in the achievement of an accurate hover over water, even in nil-visibility conditions. Hovering a helicopter accurately in such conditions is beyond the capability of the best human pilot in the world without the aid of some modern scientific and technological magic. The solutions to that problem of precisely accurate hovering and to those of many others (many a solution of one problem leading to the solving of the next) were to be found in concurrent work on both sides of the Atlantic in the late 1950s and early 1960s.

Passive Sonar

The second form of sonar, passive, has advantages and disadvantages, like almost any other of man's inventions. In essence passive sonar consists of a system of buoys which 'listen' but which do not transmit; they can be free-dropped from helicopters and fixed-wing aircraft in predetermined patterns and then left to do their jobs until having done it, they descend into a watery grave and are written off, classed as expendable by supply officers and forgotten.

The main advantage of the system is that the mute, listening buoys are totally undetectable by the opposition whereas both the outgoing signal of an active dunked buoy and the resonance of the helicopter dangling it can be picked up by an alert and well-equipped opposition submarine commander, at least giving him warning that he is being hunted, even if he knows not from precisely where. Among the disadvantages are the time and flying distances involved in covering an effective pattern and the difficulty of obtaining a precise position, justifying the launching of weapons from this means alone.

In 1974 No 814 NAS, equipped with Westland Sea Kings, began feasibility trials with American-made passive sonar equipment under the codename 'Jezebel'. These trials proved that it was a practical proposition to equip helicopters with the system but that it would be advisable to retain the active equipment on board as well. An improved form of passive sonar, which will be described in more detail later, has been fitted in the latest of the RN's Sea King 'family', the Mk 5, which is now in service in all the front-line ASW squadrons.

From the time that early trials began with the sonar-equipped Whirlwinds it was clear that another major problem, apart from that of sheer payload, had to be overcome — controllability.

Controllability

By the sheer nature of aerodynamics the helicopter totally lacks the desirable quality of 'inherent stability' and so means had to be found of making it less fatiguing to fly on long and exacting missions, and indeed possible to fly at all at night or in bad visibility, especially when it came to the essential business of hovering accurately over a featureless sea. Both sets of problems were solved down the years on both sides of the Atlantic in step with the onward march of a number of technologies.

The main contributions came from the evolution of small, lightweight turboshaft engines and the miniaturisation of numerous electronic devices, especially computers. Another basic design from the Sikorsky stable, the S-58 (HSS-1 in the USN and the Wessex in Britain, after much anglicisation by Westland) provided the stepping stone towards the true hunter-killer.

The weight-lifting problem was approached in two different ways on the opposite sides of the Atlantic. The USN went for a 'pairs' technique with its piston-powered HSS-1s, one carrying the hunting equipment, the other the weapons. In the RN an attempt was made to load both sonar and weapons into a single aircraft (the Wessex Mk 3) but the sortie length resulting was only just about viable. In all the trials, training and sometime tribulation of the 1950s and 1960s, however, a great many things slotted themselves together as if in readiness for the right airframe over the horizon.

The Sikorsky S-58 first flew on 8 March 1954 and two years later Westland obtained a licence to build the aircraft in Britain with the very important anglicisation feature of a 1,100shp Napier Gazelle turboshaft engine in place of the piston Wright R-1820-84.

Quite apart from the benefits of its power:weight ratio and reliability the turbine engine allowed for the introduction of a 'computerised' power control system giving the pilot instant and flexible command of the behaviour or his main rotor blades and eliminating the necessity for a 'third hand' manipulating a twist-grip throttle on his collective pitch lever — the one which makes a helicopter go up or down. (Hand throttles were eliminated altogether in the various Marks of Wessex but reintroduced as part of the S-61 design into the Sea King to cope with possible failures of the automatic engine control system.)

The Wessex HAS Mk 1 as delivered to the RN in 1960 was its first 'electronic helicopter', the Hawker Siddeley Dynamics (later Rolls-Royce) power control system being but one of a number of features which made the night and day, all-weather hunting of submarines a practical proposition. Since much of this 'magic' was later to form the heart of the avionics of the Sea King it is worth while describing in some detail at this stage to make later references more understandable.

A method of achieving an accurate hover over a featureless sea (the pilot of a 'simple' helicopter *must* have a visual reference in order to hover, be it a church steeple or a pair of car headlights) had been evolved in the HAS7 Whirlwinds, depending upon the sonar cable itself. In the Whirlwinds, during trials at Lee-on-Solent, a device was produced in which the cable passed between two magnetically charged forks set at right angles to each other. A sort of Maltese Cross instrument in the cockpit was provided and when the cable was properly vertical two needles crossed in the centre of the meter. Movement away from the vertical was (and still is) shown by the needles moving away from the centre point in the same direction as the cable movement. Height, in the earlier experiments, was calculated by recording the depth of the sonar body on the end of its wire. This was a sound system and in modified and improved form still constitutes the heart of ASW sonar dunking operations in the Sea King era.

The problems in the Whirlwind 7 era were that the pilot had to do almost everything manually and usually on his own because payload requirements normally precluded the presence of a helper in the left-hand seat. It was a very exhausting business indeed, not only so far as the pilot's mental endurance was concerned, but also so far as his physical limitations were concerned. There were questions of cramp in his left hand which was moving up and down the collective *and* twisting the throttle grip, and possibly some cramp in his left leg which had to maintain constant pressure on the rudder pedal to keep the thing pointing into the wind — an absolute prerequisite for accurate hovering and the vertical dunking of the sonar buoy, which it was of course all about.

Apart from the power control system two other pieces of 'avionic magic' were installed into the Wessex 1s — auto stabilisation equipment (ASE), which in a fixed-wing aviator's language would just be called 'trimming'; and perhaps most importantly a flight control system (FCS, later expanded to AFCS or automatic flight control system). Both systems were perfected by a remarkable British firm, Louis Newmark. On the other side of the Atlantic its work was matched by companies like Hamilton Standard.

Auto stabilisation equipment (now shortened in general parlance to STAB) gave helicopter pilots for the first time the ability to fly 'hands off', something which the pilots of well-mannered fixed-wing aircraft had been able to do for half a century. The helicopter being the sort of flying machine it is (some cynical airmen say the only thing wrong with it is that it does not really want to fly) requires rather more complicated kit than some tabs on ailerons, elevators and rudder and a little wheel in the cockpit to keep it straight and level in the air while the pilot attends to other matters. The trimming system is seen in the cockpit of a modern helicopter as a number of small buttons, looking like miniature black 'Chinese hats', mounted on the cyclic pitch lever (which looks like a joystick but which performs rather different functions, making the aircraft go forward or backward rather than making it dive or climb) and on the collective pitch lever (which as stated earlier makes it go up or down). STAB has taken a vast amount of strain out of the workload of any helicopter pilot, particularly out of that of a naval ASW pilot who has so many other things to consider apart from just 'driving'.

The AFCS — which later turned out to be of enormous value in difficult rescue operations — was borne out of the necessity for ASW helicopters to fly complicated patterns in all weather and visibility conditions and descend to an appropriate hovering height of about 40ft above the sea to lower their sonar buoys. The system was evolved by feeding through a computer the inputs from Doppler aerials (giving an indication of forward, backward and sideways movement, again on the reflection or echo principle) and from a radar altimeter giving a precisely accurate height reading from about 1,000ft downwards. At the pilot's end of the business an AFCS helicopter is flown by Human Brain Mk 1 (plus some assistance from radar and other navigational devices) to an appropriate point facing into wind at about 200ft altitude. A small button, appropriately marked 'Trans Down' is then pressed, whereupon AFCS will take the aircraft down to the 40ft level (about the right height from which to lower a sonar body yet remain clear of the majority of wave crests and the worst of the salt spray) and keep it there. The Maltese Cross instrument on the panel gives the pilot or pilots a check reading on the accuracy of the hover. Once the buoy is lowered the system evolved earlier of the magnetic gate comes into play again, refining still further the accuracy of the hover to within a knot or two in any direction. When a dunking task is completed and it is time to move on to another corner of the sea, another button, equally appropriately marked 'Trans Up' is pressed and all concerned ascend to the 200ft altitude whereupon human brains take over again.

The FCS in the Wessex 1 was Simplex with no duplication of electronics or wiring and did have to be carefully monitored. In the Wessex 3, which contained many other improvements, it was made Duplex with fail-safe back-ups for everything, but by the time of arrival of the Sea King in FAA hands the Louis Newmark system had become so well proven that it went back to Simplex again and has seldom been known to fail.

Those were the internal ingredients available for the RN's first true submarine hunter-killer helicopter, urgently needed by the early 1960s. There had been a brief flirtation with the idea of developing the British designed Bristol 173 twin-rotor helicopter but in response to a 1957 US Navy requirement the aeroplane called the Sikorsky S-61 had first flown on 11 March 1959 and there was really nothing else in the Western world to match it. Although Americans seem to dislike naming their aircraft but bestow on them a bewildering variety of initial letters and numbers, somebody in the sales department of Sikorsky's dubbed this one 'Sea King', and it became a name with which to conjure.

Right: Interseat console layout. *Westland*

Interseat Console Layout

1 — Compass Control Unit GM9 System; **2** — VHF/UHF AM/FM Collins AN/ARC 182; **3** — Vertical Gyro Switch Box; **4** — AFCS Controller Engage Lights Dim; **5** — Null Indicator; **6** — ASE Controller; **7** — Decca TANS 9447 Computer; **8** — ASE Channel Selector; **9** — Racal Acoustics Audio Selector Unit; **10** — Racal Acoustics I/C Station Box; **11** — VOR/ILS and VHF Control Unit; **12** — Marconi AD380S ADF Controller; **13** — Marconi AD380S ADF Distress Frequency Selector; **14** — IFF Cossor 2720 Control Unit; **15** — Auxiliary Flotation Control Unit; **16** — Armament Panel — Exocet Fire (and Jettison All); **17** — Blanking Plate; **18** — Racal Acoustics Audio Selector Unit; **19** — Racal Acoustics I/C Station Box; **20** — Radio Selector Box; **21** — Collins HF 718-U5; **22** — Guns/Rockets Selector Unit; **23** — Rocket Control Panels; **24** — Armament Panel (MASS); **25** — Gyro Master Switch Box.

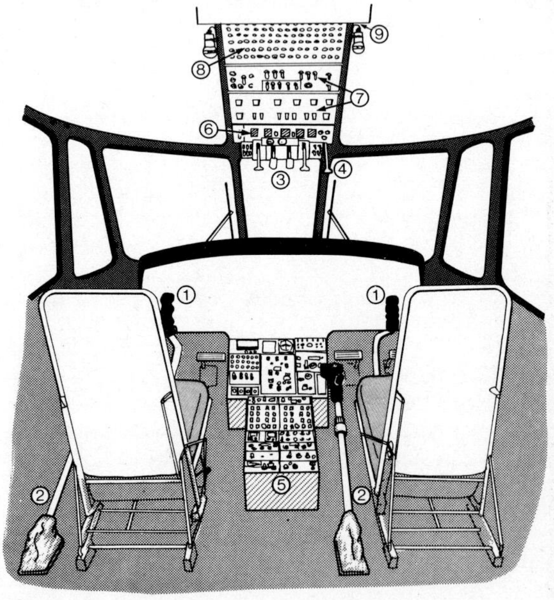

Right: Diagrammatic representation of a typical Sea King cockpit. *Bob Downey*

1 Cycle Sticks
2 Collective Pitch Levers
3 Engine Controls
4 Rotor Brake
5 Interseat Console
6 Emergency Panel
7 Lighting and Miscellaneous Panels
8 Circuit Breaker Panel
9 Cabin Dome Light Panel

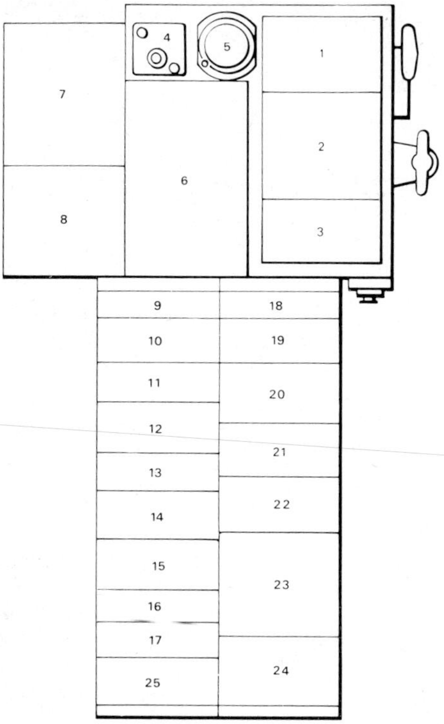

Typical Instrument Panel Layout

1 — Air Speed Indicators; **2** — Standby Attitude Indicator; **3** — Barometric Altimeter; **4** — Main Attitude Indicators with Director Bars; **5** — Horizontal Situation Indicator; **6** — Radar Altimeter Indicators; **7** — Hover Indicators; **8** — Rate of Climb Indicators; **9** — Cruise Guide Indicators; **10** — Dual Torque Meter Indicators; **11** — Combined Triple Tachometer Indicators; **12** — Fuel Contents Indicator (Forward); **13** — Fuel Contents Indicator (Aft); **14** — Gas Generator Tachometer Indicator (No 1 Engine); **15** — Gas Generator Tachometer Indicator (No 2 Engine); **16** — Power Turbine Inlet Temperature Indicator (No 1 Engine); **17** — Power Turbine Inlet Temperature Indicator (No 2 Engine); **18** — Engine Oil Pressure Indicator (No 1 Engine); **19** — Engine Oil Pressure Indicator (No 2 Engine); **20** — Engine Oil Temperature Indicator (No 1 Engine); **21** — Engine Oil Temperature Indicator (No 2 Engine); **22** — Transmission Oil Pressure Indicator; **23** — Transmission Oil Temperature Indicator; **24** — Auxiliary Hydraulic Pressure Indicator; **25** — Primary Hydraulic Pressure Indicator; **26** — Utility Hydraulic Pressure Indicator; **27** — Time Elapsed Clock; **28** — Exocet Target Range Indicator.

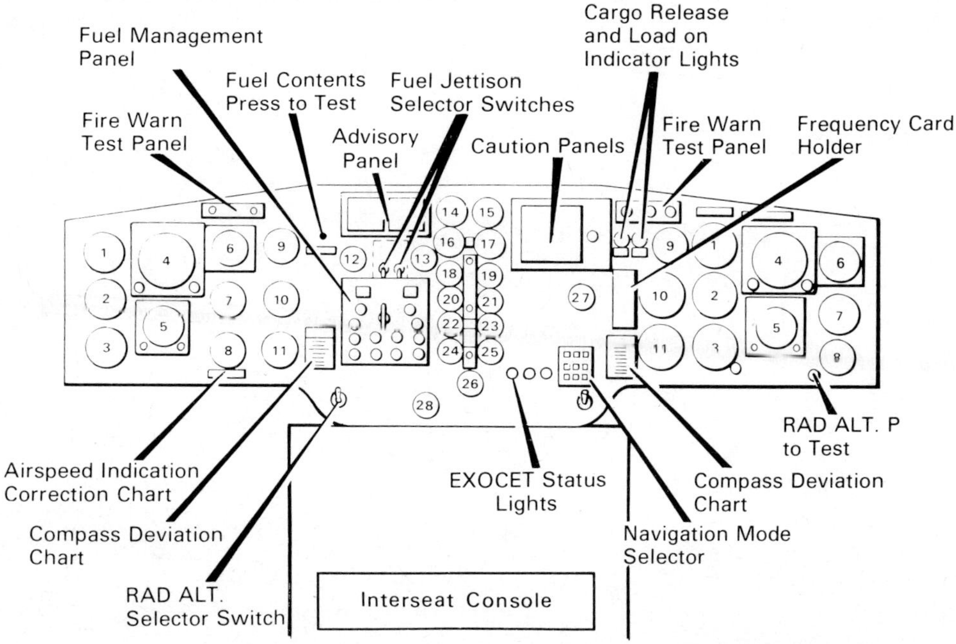

Typical instrument panel layout. *Westland*

farthing' principle perfected by Igor Sikorksy in the VS300 20 years earlier, and proven as reliable even if some power was still diverted away from pure lift — in contrast to the contra-rotating twin main rotor concept to be eventually proved in the Chinooks of a few years later.

An important departure in the S-61 design was the provision for a two-pilot flightdeck and a level hull behind, along which all members of the crew could walk and talk. This contrasted with the S-55 (Whirlwind) and S-58 (Wessex) configurations in which it was possible for two pilots to be alongside each other 'upstairs' but in which it was frequently necessary for someone to descend acrobatically backwards into the 'back end' to work a rescue winch or assist with the sonar gear, trying very hard in the process *not* to kick the pilot's cyclic stick out of his hands.

The sponsons at each side of the fuselage, were designed to act as floats as well as housings for the retractable main landing wheels and could also be made mounting points for torpedoes, depth charges, machine guns and additional flotation bags.

The USN gave Sikorsky a contract for the S-61 project on Christmas Eve 1957 and awarded the aircraft the designation HSS-2. It was under this label that the aircraft first flew 15 months later. The design was redesignated SH-3A in the USN in July 1962 when the American armed forces accepted a new tri-service system for marking their aircraft. (It will probably be simpler for all concerned if I refer to American-built Sea Kings as H-3s when in military service on that side of the Atlantic. SH in USN terminology stands for Search, roughly equivalent in RN terminology to HAS, standing for Helicopter Anti-Submarine. From henceforward the civilian (US-built) versions of the aircraft will be referred to under the Sikorsky original 'S-61' designation with appropriate final letters, and the Westland-built aircraft as Sea Kings with Mk numbers added.)

The twin-engine reliability and increased range and payload of the SH-3A were immediate and important advances for the USN's AS operations but some internal developments were also clearly needed. The early AN/AQS-4 sonar as used in the S-55 and S-58 series of helicopters only gave a 10° wide search beam and a full traverse could occupy the crew for five minutes or more of exhausting and demanding flying during which a wily opponent might escape.

Bendix developed an improved sonar system, the AQS-10, specifically for the SH-3A. This had a wider beam and could traverse through 360° within a minute. This improved sonar, together with the American version of the AFCS (using a Ryan APN-130 Doppler radar and a radar altimeter) plus automatic stabilisation (STAB) developed by Hamilton Standard were stitched together to make the SH-3 a true all-weather 24hr hunter-killer; soon after its introduction Sikorsky's claimed that the aircraft represented in financial terms four times the value of an S-58.

After two years of particularly exhaustive trials and tests the USN received its first SH-3As in 1961, initially operating them from bases at Key West, Norfolk (Virginia) and San Diego. At about this time too Sikorsky set up a world helicopter speed record of

Left: The first S-61A delivered to the USAF on 23 March 1962. *Sikorsky*

Right: A 'bombed-up' S-61A on test. *Sikorsky*

210.6mph in a Sea King — the first aircraft of this configuration to exceed 200mph.

More than 200 SH-3As were built for the USN. The first of them were powered by the 1,050shp version of the General Electric T58-GE-6 soon to be up-rated to 1,250shp, providing for a gross weight of 19,100lb (8,664kg) compared with the original 18,000lb (8,165kg).

The next major forward step was the introduction of the SH-3D, which was to become the model upon which the Westland Mk 1 Sea King was to be based. The SH-3D was fitted with the more potent T58-GE-10 engines each capable of delivering 1,400shp. In common with the up-powering of all helicopters this necessitated an improved and stronger gearbox. Other improvements between 3A and 3D included an improved sonar system, the AQS-13-A and an APN182 Doppler in place of the 180. Gross weight went up to 20,500lb (9,300kg) and some strengthening of the fuselage structure was called for. The USN received a total of 74 SH-3Ds.

Many other variations on the theme of the basic S-61 design emerged in the 1960s including VIP transports frequently used by Presidents of the United States seen making frequent television appearances. (A hilarious shot showing the forward port side door of one with its built-in stepladder dropping on the heads of two red-carpet layers has been carefully preserved in archives). Some USN aircraft were modified for mine countermeasures duties, and importantly 12 3As, designated HH-3A, were used for Search and Rescue duties in Vietnam. (HH stands for Rescue in US terminology.)

The USAF began using the aircraft type in 1962 with H-3s borrowed from the Navy and adapted as 27-seat troop carriers — a foretaste of Westlands development of the Commando or Mk 4 version of its Sea King.

A land combat version, first labelled the S-61R, was evolved with its float sponsons substituted by lifting aerofoil stub wings and a hydraulically operated rear door and loading ramp incorporated. This type was first designated CH(Cargo Helicopter)-3C, then with up-rated engines CH-3E.

A further modification of this type designated HH-3E and carrying armour plate protection for the crew together with defensive machine guns went into action in Vietnam from 1966 onwards. This was the model which earned the affectionate appelation of 'Jolly Green Giant' from grateful ground troops and downed airmen, the allusion being to a well-known brand of that staple item of the American diet, the canned bean. (The larger HH-53Cs, some of which are stationed in the UK at Woodbridge, Suffolk, are properly styled 'Super Jolly Green Giants'.)

In parallel with the military developments Sikorsky was in a financial position to promote the basic design into the civilian world and it was in this guise that the aircraft 'shape' first became familiar to the British public, although television audiences had already admired Sea Kings carrying out astronaut recovery operations after splashdowns while bearing such intriguing callsigns as 'Swim One', 'Recovery One' and 'Photo One'.

The first commercial versions were offered as landplanes (S-61Ls) with fixed undercarriages in place

Top right: A land combat CH-3 version of the S-61 basic design. *Sikorsky*

Right: A typical instance of how the 'Sea King shape' became familiar to the British public in the late 1960s. An SH-3D from USS *Hornet* picking up Apollo 12 astronauts Richard Gordon and Allen Bean as they leave their command module after splash-down in the South Pacific on 24 November 1969. *Sikorsky*

Below: One of the first commercial S-61s — a landplane version bought by Los Angeles Airways. *Sikorsky*

Right: A British Airways S-61N taking off from Penzance on the now well-established Scilly Islands service.

Below: A Bristow S-61N, typical of many used on the North Sea oil rig services. *Sikorsky*

of the sponsons and accommodation for 28 passengers. This particular member of the family has only had limited success, however, and it has been the S-61N version, reverting to float sponsons, (rather bigger ones than those fitted to the naval aircraft) which has made a substantial impact on the world at large.

The British involvement began as early as January 1964 when an S-61N, still carrying its American registration N4604G, but painted in the then British European Airways livery, was shipped to Southampton docks, assembled and flown to Gatwick. It was fairly quickly reregistered as G-ASNL. A second aircraft, G-ASNM, arrived in February and BEA inaugurated a passenger helicopter service between Penzance and the Scillies on 2 May 1964 which operated without let or hindrance until the disaster of July 1983 in which 20 people died. The BEA (later BA) S-61s, to be followed by many more operated by Bristow and other commercial companies, were destined to make an indelible mark on the conduct of the North Sea oil operations, not least in the field of rescue.

Apart from Westland, other licensees of the S-61 design were to be Mitsubishi Heavy Industries, Japan, and Costruzioni Aeronautiche Giovanni Augusta in Italy, the latter company to enter into fundamentally important partnership arrangements with Britain in the whole helicopter world.

In January 1983 Sikorsky recorded that there were 443 military S-61s operating worldwide with more than 2million flight-hours accumulated. The 112 commercial S-61s had by then amassed nearly one million flight-hours at a rate of about 100,000 hours per year. The company claimed that the 'Commercials' had by then flown more passengers more miles than any other helicopter and three times as many hours under instrument flight rules than all other commercial helicopters combined.

This then, was the broad background to the position in the mid-1960s when the RN so urgently needed its effective submarine hunter-killer helicopters. The British helicopter manufacturing industry, 'rationalised' under the notorious 1957 Defence White Paper, had nothing satisfactory on offer, although it *had* nearly had a winner several years earlier in the form of a Bristol-designed tandem-rotor aircraft, originally called the Bristol 173, moving through various designations to the 192 and to the Bristol (and/or Westland) Belvedere as used by the RAF with moderate success.

The FAA had had its eyes on this design from as far back as 1953 when a 173 was handed over to the Admiralty for trials on board HMS *Eagle.* Three years later the Navy actually placed an order for 68 aircraft, to be known as 191s, with folding rotor blades and shortened fuselages so that they could fit into existing carrier lifts, and with modified rear undercarriages making them capable of carrying torpedoes. Politics, and some technical problems, brought a sad end to this project and the Navy had to look across the Atlantic again and inevitably the eyes of procurement officers turned to the well proven S-61 or H-3 design.

The deal was made on 27 June 1966 — Westland was to build 60 Sea Kings at a fixed price of £24million, at that time the largest single contract ever obtained by the company, which had entered the aviation business in 1915 as James B. Petter & Sons, manufacturers of oil engines for the agricultural industry, and anxious to help in the war effort. (Curiously, in the light of current events, it was James B. Petter which had built the only aircraft to participate in the Battle of Jutland, a Short 184 Seaplane, No 8359, piloted by Lt J. F. Rutland with Assistant Paymaster G. S. Trewin as his Observer, which scouted for Sir David Beatty's Battle Cruiser Fleet and spotted a strong enemy force before low cloud forced it back to land. Curiously too, the ship they were embarked on was HMS *Engadine*, a name to be perpetuated in the early development of the Sea King and the training of most Sea King crews as that of the Royal Fleet Auxiliary (RFA) helicopter training ship which is still in service and which performed gallantly in the Falklands.)

In spite of the fact that after the aircraft industry rationalisation Westland had emerged as the sole major builder of helicopters in Britain there was still an element of competition over the Sea King contract. Sikorsky did try quite hard to sell its aircraft directly to the British government but at the same time made an agreement to allow Westland to build under licence if the latter organisation offered a deal more acceptable to the British public. In the event the Westland bid succeeded not only on straightforward financial grounds but for the important political reason that a British firm, employing British workers, would be seen to be making one of the nation's most important aircraft. In addition the S-61/H-3 was to be anglicised so far as almost all its internal components were concerned. In equine terms it might have been fair to describe the resultant aircraft as 'by Sikorsky out of Westland' — or perhaps the other way round?

Below: One of the first of the many — an early HSS-2 (or H-3) of the USN demonstrating the hunter-killer's potential and also its downwash. *Sikorsky*

Birth of the Westland Sea King

In October 1966 the first of four 'pattern' aircraft, purchased from Sikorsky, arrived at Avonmouth docks. It bore the British civil registration G-ATYU, was in maker's designation an S-61D-2 and was given the British service airframe serial number XV370. It was assembled on the dockside and flown to the Westland factory at Yeovil by the company's chief test pilot, Mr 'Slim' Sear.

Three other aircraft (XV371, XV372 and XV373) were delivered in kit form. For about three months XV370 was flown on performance trials with its General Electric T58 engines and other American equipment, then stripped down in readiness for its systems development role and anglicisation but still retaining its American engines for a further period.

Ostensibly the most important anglicisation feature in the first four development aircraft was the substitution of the British Gnome engines for the GE turboshafts, though it has to be recorded that the now world famous Gnome, first built under the de Havilland label at Leavesden, Watford (subsequently under Bristol Siddeley and eventually Rolls-Royce trademarks) was in fact a licensee 'job' from General Electric in the first place. That small point having been recorded should in no way be taken as any denigration of the skill and effort put into the manufacture and subsequent up-grading of the Gnome engine at Leavesden, particularly when the factory there (long noted for its production of de Havilland Gipsy engines) finally settled under Rolls-Royce management.

By the time the first Sea King airframe kits had arrived at Yeovil, Rolls-Royce Gnome H1400 engines with a $2\frac{1}{2}$-minute contingency rating of 1,500shp, a one-hour maximum rating of 1,400shp and a continuous 1,250shp rating were available, together with the 'full authority' Hawker Siddeley Dynamics/Rolls-Royce electronic engine control system which was regarded as an advance on the Hamilton Standard electro-mechanical system fitted to the GE T58s.

Above: A 'Westland selection'. From top to bottom: an RN Mk 5; an RN Mk 4; an RAF HAR3; and RN Mk 2; and a Mk 1 (XV373) in Boscombe Down colours. *Westland*

Left: Sea King XV371, bearing Royal Aircraft Establishment insignia, flying over Britain c1967. *RAE Farnborough*

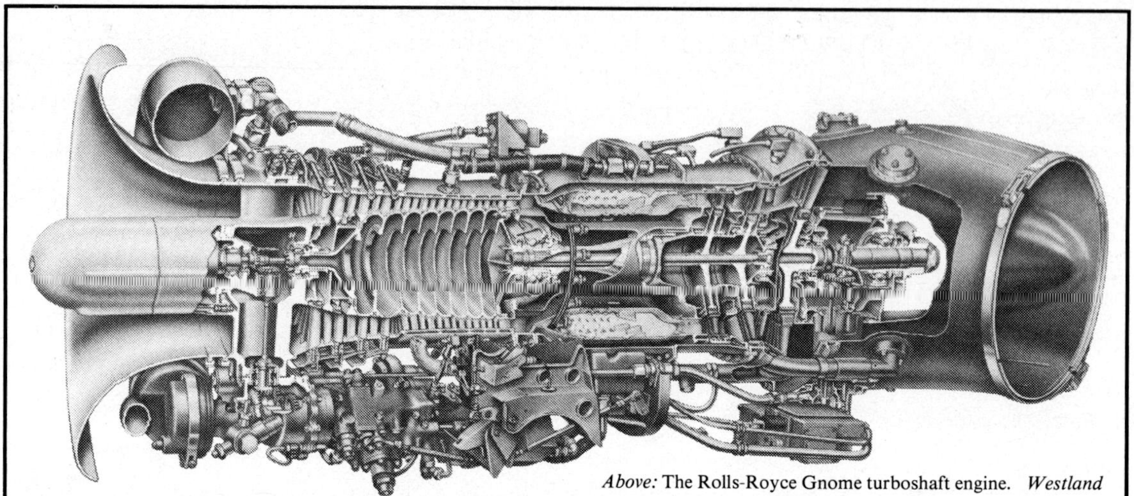

Above: The Rolls-Royce Gnome turboshaft engine. *Westland*

The Gnome engines, subsequently to be up-graded several times, had a 10-stage axial flow compressor, an annular combustion chamber, a two-stage axial flow gas generator turbine and a three single-stage power turbine.

The pattern aircraft, and subsequently the production Westland Sea King Mk 1s, had light alloy main rotor blades with extruded leading edges and 23 fabricated pockets bonded to the main spars. Inert gas was fed into the rotor blades under pressure, thus enabling a cockpit reading to be taken to indicate any incipient failure — a facility which was to prove useful many years later when some Sea King blades were punctured by Argentinian cannon shells.

After being fitted with Gnome engines XV370 'first flew' again on 8 September 1967 as the first anglicised Sea King. Unfortunately XV372 which was assigned to Rolls-Royce for engine development flying crashed in January 1969 on a flight between Bristol and Yeovil following an engine flame-out caused by ice ingestion and an unsuccessful attempt by the crew to pull off a smooth auto-rotation landing, an event which was to lead to a considerable amount of drawing board study and thereby an improvement of the breed.

'The first of the many' XV370 was, at the time of writing, still flying from the Royal Aircraft & Armament Experimental Establishment, Boscombe Down in the Empire Test Pilots' School and in proud red, white

Left: Five Sea Kings of the RN's Intensive Flying Trials Unit (No 700S Squadron) showing its paces in 1969. *RN*

Right: The Royal Navy has many Sea Kings. A Mk 1 is properly dressed, with others, for entering harbour at Plymouth. *Westland*

and blue colours. No XV371 was still on development work at the Royal Aircraft Establishment, Farnborough; and XV373 at RAE Bedford. The hulk of XV372 was still being used by Westland at Yeovil for various mysterious experiments and had therefore not exactly died in vain.

The first of the 56 production Westland Mk 1 Sea Kings for the RN, No XV642, flew from Yeovil on 7 May 1969. Two months later the first deck landing by the type was made on to the apparently immortal RFA *Engadine* by Lt-Cdr C. J. Horscroft and Lt P. J. G. Harper from the Aircraft Handling Squadron, Boscombe Down.

Another Intensive Flying Trials Unit, this time styled No 700S NAS, was commissioned on 19 August 1969 and achieved the task of proving six aircraft 'in all respects' through 2,700 hours in a period slightly short of the allotted nine months.

The aircraft the Squadron was invited to test, while by no means a new type, did differ widely from the already proven American H-3. In fact it is sometimes claimed that only the airframe and the rotor head system were precisely the same although the purchase arrangement had been officially classified as 'minimum change', perhaps to satisfy cost-conscious politicians of the day.

The RN's ASW techniques evolved in the Whirlwind and Wessex eras had led especially to a different crewing arrangement from that adopted on the other side of the Atlantic. One essential feature was that the Observer, always a commissioned officer in an RN ASW helicopter, had become rated as the 'tactical co-ordinator' or 'anti-submarine officer', capable of taking full control of a search and attack operation independently of accompanying surface ships frequently commanded by officers of much higher rank. Thus in an RN Sea King the first pilot in the right hand seat might well be regarded as 'The Master of the Vessel' in sailing ship terms; the captain of the aircraft could be the Observer officer, usually sitting in the

Partly because of the low altitude at which most operations are carried out, helicopters do not show up well on radar screens and MEL transponders were fitted as well as IFF (Identification Friend or Foe).

Some security restrictions apply on the detail of weapon loads, but from the start the Navy was loading mixes of homing torpedoes and depth charges or full loads of one or the other, according to task.

Westland Sea King XV645 was collected from Yeovil on 11 August 1969 by the CO designate of No 700S Squadron (the Intensive Flying Trials Unit), Lt-Cdr Victor Sirett, and flown by him to RNAS Culdrose. By Commissioning Day on 19 August two more aircraft, XV644 and XV646, had been delivered and Culdrose had become the natural home of the RN's Sea Kings.

'Vic' Sirett had already played a significant part in the development of naval helicopters which could carry out their essential tasks of flying, and more importantly, hovering, in all conditions of weather and visibility. He had been involved in some of the earliest trials at Lee-on-Solent and at Culdrose which had led to this desirable end-product.

In 1963 the then Lt Vic Sirett, duty Wessex SAR pilot on board HMS *Ark Royal* steaming in the Gulf of Aden, was called with his crew to search for and rescue the survivors of a Sea Vixen which had ditched. He pulled the job off, applying many techniques he had himself helped to evolve, using the 'cable mode' of achieving a precise hover over the ditched pilot in his dinghy in spite of it being a very dark night ('like a witch's tit' was his own description). The rescue was nearly spoiled by the understandable over-enthusiasm of the Vixen pilot who swam out of his dinghy and first grabbed the sonar buoy cable instead of the rescue hoist wire, but it all worked out in the end. The Sea Vixen's Observer was rescued by a surface ship a little later but the important thing was that Lt Sirett had proved that helicopter rescues involving precise hovering could be carried out at night.

Again with much foresight the Lords of the Admiralty sent Lt-Cdr Sirett out on attachment to Air Development Squadron One at the USN Air Station Key West, Florida in the mid-1960s to obtain experience on a helicopter called the SH-3. While he was there Vic Sirett was involved in two live rescues and collected two awards. On 22 December he was co-pilot of SH-3A No 148052 on a routine instrument training flight when his aircraft was diverted to assist two downed USAF F-102 pilots who had collided over the Gulf of Mexico. A Letter of Commendation from the Development Squadron's CO said that Lt-Cdr Sirett's skill controlling the helicopter during one rescue and his assistance to the aircraft commander in the second, 'contributed immeasurably to the expeditious and safe recovery of two pilots'. Vic Sirett also received the 'Winged S' Air Rescue Emblem from Sikorsky for 'skill and courage in a lifesaving mission with a Sikorsky helicopter'.

The formidable tasks with which Lt-Cdr Sirett and No 700S Squadron were charged involved five out of six aircraft carrying out 400 hours each in the primary ASW role, the sixth aircraft to concentrate on 700 hours of other types of flying. The ASW trials were to include 1,300 hours of day and night sonar dunking and 400 hours AS screening and navigation.

Left: The commissioning ceremony of No 700S Squadron at Culdrose on 19 August 1969 — XV645 in the background. *RN*

Above right and right: XV645 lifting a 105mm howitzer and jeep, a total weight of three tons — and a 48ft bridge. *Westland*

The aircraft allocated to the Squadron were airframe Nos XV644 to XV649, bearing 'pennant numbers' 582 to 587 plus code letters CU for Culdrose on their tail rotor pylons. The secondary roles to be explored included SAR, deck landings, underslung load carrying, conversion to troop carrying, photography and the mounting and use of defensive general purpose machine guns. The 'Permitted failures' laid down by the Ministry of Technology were 13 for the automatic flight control system, 46 for the engines and 180 for the airframes.

Assisting Lt-Cdr Sirett were Senior Pilot, Lt-Cdr H. Foster; Senior Observer, Lt-Cdr R. Flindell; Engineer Officer, Lt-Cdr R. Hillsden; Electrical Officer, Lt-Cdr P. Cushion; Assistant Engineer Officer Lt B. Sargent; and Assistant Engineer Officer, Lt G. R. Woodcock. The remainder of the Squadron complement was made up of 12 pilots, six observers and 97 ratings.

The first task was converting the 12 pilots to Sea King handling techniques but it was appreciated from the start that the trials programme would differ from

Above: A Sea King helping to preserve history.

Left: Sea King HAS5 off the Cornish coast. *Westland*

any others carried out previously by the FAA in that the Sea King was to be assessed as a complete weapons system, not just a new type of aircraft.

Before 700S Squadron began its task Westland had carried out 160 hours of trials in two weeks and coincidentally with the 700S programme the company carried out 1,500 hours of its own development flying. In the event the 700S programme was completed three weeks ahead of schedule and the defects recorded amounted to 33% of the permitted 13 in the flight control system; 16% of the permitted 46 for the engines and 25% of the permitted 180 for the airframe. The six aircraft completed an average of 468¼ flying hours each with an average maintenance period of 4.9 hours of flying.

To everybody's intense pride the coveted Boyd Trophy for the year 1970 was awarded to the Squadron and the citation addressed to Lt-Cdr Sirett read:

'The determined manner in which he went about this task, his enthusiasm and personal leadership, ensured that at all times the morale and humour of his men remained at the highest level despite constant demands, late work and frequent setbacks. In the event the Intensive Flying Trials Unit achieved every aspect of its programmed task on time and did so with consummate professionalism.

'Not only was the Sea King proven in its ASW role but equally evaluated in its secondary support role. This has clearly been a vital factor in the Sea King's subsequent successful performance with the Fleet.'

This was an auspicious start.

Naturally there had been some moments of drama however. The 700S Squadron record mentions that on 27 August 1969, the day of the very first dunking exercises, XV644 returned from a sortie unable to lock the undercarriage down. The wheels were eventually locked down by ground crew as the aircraft hovered over the hard standing and a safe landing was made — thus proving another advantage which the helicopter has over fixed-wing aircraft in certain times of 'distress'. The following day XV646 returned on one engine from Falmouth Bay. The offending (port) engine was removed and Rolls-Royce was called in to deal with the problem.

On 6 October 1970 a visit by the Australian Helicopter Evaluation Mission was recorded — a significant event in the light of future overseas sales and the on-going development of the Sea King, and on 15 July a Norwegian Defence Department Mission visited the Squadron to examine the Sea King's potential in the SAR role, another important pointer towards the future.

Indeed, the potential of the aircraft in the SAR role was proved several times during the Intensive Flying Trials. On 3 May 1970 eight Sea Kings, four from No 700S Squadron and four from No 824 NAS (which had just been formed by then as the first front-line unit to employ the aircraft), set off on a routine detachment flight to Lossiemouth in Northern Scotland. They were diverted to Portland initially to assist in the search for the crew of a Phantom, missing from HMS *Ark Royal*, but after 3½ hours works the task was called off and they continued to Lossiemouth.

On 14 May 1970 a Sea King from No 700S Squadron created a record by flying the longest distance recorded during a UK rescue operation up to that date to pick up a seriously ill seaman from the Finnish tanker *Tiskeri* about 170 miles southwest of Land's End (200 miles from Culdrose). The weather was good and the Sea King was assisted in locating the tanker by an RAF Shackleton. In this small, almost unnoticed, incident the potential of the aircraft to save life at long distances was proved; also the technique of co-operation between long range helicopters and the RAF's maritime reconnaissance aircraft — at that stage Shackletons, soon to be replaced by Nimrods.

Just over a year later the life-saving ability was to be proved again when two Mk 1 Sea Kings of No 824 NAS took off from Culdrose on the morning of 18 October 1971 to assist the crew of the 10,800ton Norwegian bulk carrier *Anatina*, on fire in a gale more than 200 miles away to the west. The two helicopters flew a record long distance non-stop return flight of 430 miles in a Force 9 severe gale to drop supplies of blankets, fresh water, clothing and hot food to the captain and nine crew members who stayed aboard to winch 11 others off the ship.

Just before the 700S Squadron trials task was due to end Lt-Cdr Sirett notched up another cheerful event in his familiar style of panache. He flew XV649 (pennant No 87) from Land's End to John O'Groats in 4hr 19min 22sec, thereby establishing the longest recorded nonstop flight by a British Services helicopter, over a distance of 602.95 miles at an average speed of 139.49mph. To add a little more tone to the occasion he took some 'official flown covers' with him for the philatelists and after over-flying John O'Groats he landed to refuel at Lossiemouth and was presented with a haggis on a silver salver by the RNAS staff there.

Coincidentally with the later stages of the 700S Squadron trials, No 824 NAS was commissioned at Culdrose in February 1970 under the command of Lt-Cdr L. Hallett. A number of aircrew and 'maintainers' from No 700S Squadron were transferred to the new unit. No 824 NAS was destined to take its Sea Kings on board HMS *Ark Royal* and remain with that famous ship until the end of its last

Above: The scene millions of viewers of the TV series *Sailor* will remember. While an episode for the programme about HMS *Ark Royal* was being filmed one of the ship's Sea Kings went to the rescue of a seriously ill crewman on the American submarine *Bergal*. While the stretcher was being hooked on a rogue wave swept the sick man and his rescuer, CPO Aircrewman Roy Withell into the sea. Both were winched to safety and CPO Withell was awarded the Queen's Gallantry Medal.
Leading Airman Steve Collinson/RN

Left: Lt-Cdr Sirett receives his haggis after setting up a long-distance helicopter record. *RN*

Above right: Sonar dunking practice by No 706 Squadron aircraft. *RN*

commission. The Squadron remains in existence, still equipped with Sea Kings to the present day, but normally embarked on board vessels of the RFA.

In April 1970 No 700S Squadron began converting pilots from No 826 NAS on to the Sea King and at the beginning of May a detachment was established at Lossiemouth to 'progress the evaluation of the Sea King in the context of the fast submarine'. Some typically laconic remarks enliven the last page of the 'S 1216 H' Squadron Record Form for No 700S Squadron in May 1970. Floral Day in Helston was put down as 'Sunday Routine'. The period 25-29 May was recalled as a week starting well with a Bank Holiday and the Queen's Birthday. On 26 May one aircraft flew to Ypenburg, Holland to attend an international SAR competition.

On 27 May the IFTU began a slow run-down to be completed on 29 May when the Squadron was officially disbanded. The diarist typed 'Finis. QED'.

It was not really a finis though, more a beginning for the Sea King in the RN and it should be noted that at about that time it was known that Russia was operating nearly 300 conventional and 80 nuclear submarines with the production of 'Y' class vessels equipped with SS-N-6 missiles for submerged firing running at the rate of nearly 10 per year.

The FAA was also facing up to the fact that it was probably going to lose its fixed-wing role with the impending decommissioning of *Ark Royal* — the Sea Harrier concept at that stage still being the subject of much unpromising political argument. In the spring of 1970 therefore the FAA had in the Sea King its main hope for the future; the British nation, without perhaps knowing it, had in its hands one of its most important instruments for the preservation of peace, one which 12 years later was going to help it win a totally unexpected war.

In the early 1970s the first 56 production Mk 1 Sea Kings (numbered from XV642 onwards) were deployed to five front-line naval air squadrons and to two second-line training units. Of the front-line squadrons No 824 was to have a relatively permanent 'mother' in HMS *Ark Royal* for eight years. No 819 had even more stability, being permanently shore-based at Prestwick from soon after its commissioning in February 1972 to the present day.

Nos 814, 820 and 826 Squadrons were to have more nomadic existences as ships were converted, placed in reserve or commissioned from new. After initially being embarked in HMS *Hermes* (from which its aircraft carried out a remarkable civilian evacuation task during the Cyprus troubles in 1974) No 814 was into trouble over the inhospitable Baltic and North Seas.

The aircraft ordered by the West German navy were designated Mk 41s. (Even the Mark numbers of the Westland-built Sea Kings can be confusing since many of the numbers used relate only to individual clients' requirements on quite small matters such as radio frequency channels and interior fits. An attempt will be made in this chapter to marry them up with the five distinctive UK versions of the aircraft, the RN's Mk 1, Mk 2 and Mk 5 ASW variants, its troop-carrying Mk 4, and the RAF's Mk 3 specific SAR type. The very last variant, up to the time of writing, the 'bubble-gum' Sea King carrying Airborne Early Warning (AEW) radar, had not even been given a specific Mark number, having been hastily conceived and built during the Falklands conflict.)

The Mk 41s built for Germany were equipped with much the same navigation and radar equipment as found in the RN's Mk 1s but all the sonar gear was removed and with it the 'cable-mode' hover facility in the AFCS. Additional equipment fitted related to the SAR requirement of searching for very small objects — as small as a human head — in a boundless sea. It included the Decca Mk 19 navigator, VOR/ILS (VHF omni-directional range/instrument landing system), ADF370 (automatic direction finding) radio compass and a pack of communication radios compatible with West German ground and air frequencies. The cabin heating system was beefed up — an important feature in SAR operations when survivors are frequently suffering from hypothermia — and an additional fuel tank was fitted to provide for a total of 800 (Imperial) gallons.

The first of the German Mk 41s did not in fact fly until March 1972 but this version was to become the pattern for all the SAR Sea Kings which were to make such an impact upon people at large, when used by the Royal Norwegian Air Force, the Belgian Air Force, and of course, No 202 Squadron RAF.

The German aircraft were side-numbered 8950 to 8971 with airframe numbers WA744, WA745, and WA756-WA775. One of them (WA765) was written off in January 1974 and replaced the following July by WA830. They were painted grey with red on the nose, over a fuselage band and on the rotor pylon tip, the word Marine and the letters SAR in large characters, and the side numbers split either side of the national black cross symbol.

The second overseas order, from the Indian Navy, was placed towards the end of 1969, initially for six ASW Mk 42s, basically identical with the Royal Navy's Mk 1s, but with nationally compatible communications radio and improved hot climate ventilation equipment. The first Indian aircraft flew in October 1970, six were delivered by October 1971, another three ordered in July 1972 and a further three in May 1973; finally yet another batch of three designated Mk 42As. The 15 Indian aircraft are normally based at Cochin when not embarked in ships and are operated by Indian Naval Air Squadrons Nos 30 and 336. The aircraft were allocated serial numbers IN510 onwards and painted dull blue with white topsides.

The next (third) contract, from Norway, was placed in December 1970 for 10 SAR aircraft designated Mk 43s. They were basically similar to the West German Mk 41s but with slightly reduced communications radio equipment. The first Norwegian Sea King flew in May 1972. One was lost in April 1977 on a training mission from Sola air base and was replaced. Norwegian rescue Sea Kings are painted gloss white with red noses, side flashes and radar pylons. The serial numbers are WA746 to WA755 and side numbers 060, 062, 066 and 068 to 074 are painted in black on the fuselage together with the word Redningstjeneste.

The fourth order placed in May 1973 by the Royal Australian Navy was to have an important bearing on the whole development of the Sea King because of a 'hot and high' performance requirement. This was achieved by the installation of Gnome 1400-1 engines each with a maximum continuous rating of 1,250shp, a one-hour maximum of 1,535shp and a $2\frac{1}{2}$min contingency of 1,660shp. These engines provided for an increased gross weight of 21,000lb (9.525kg), 500lb up on that of the RN's Mk 1 Sea King. They naturally required a stronger gearbox and a six-bladed tail rotor was designed in place of the original Sikorsky-designed five-bladed one to give adequate directional control under the added urge. The aircraft were also fitted with a winchable in-flight refuelling system giving them the facility to take in fuel from a ship's deck without landing. This was a significant advance, enabling Sea Kings in action well away from their own 'mother' to top up from frigates and other small ships and to keep flying even if their 'own' deck was obstructed by other aircraft. (This system must not, of course, be confused with true in-flight refuelling from another aircraft. In the helicopter world of the West this has only so far been achieved by the American forces, particularly the 'Super Jolly Green Giants' of the Aerospace Rescue & Recovery Service which have a worldwide responsibility and are fitted with telescopic probes via

Above right: A Royal Australian Navy Mk 50 recovering its sonar body. *Westland*

Right: In-flight refuelling from HMS *Tiger*. The system was first evolved from the RAN aircraft but the picture shows an RN Sea King. Note that it is important for the deck crew to position themselves on the outside of the loop in the pipe for obvious reasons. *Westland*

04
NAVY

4 2

which they can refuel from HC-130 (Hercules) tankers. The procedure remains hazardous because the average helicopter's maximum speed is only slightly above the stalling speed of a laden tanker, the rotor blades come in close proximity with the tanker's tail and for tactical reasons the task normally has to be carried out at low altitude. It is not a popular form of exercise among the crews involved.)

Some improvements in avionics were also introduced into the RAN aircraft (designated Mk 50) and this version later became the pattern for the RN's Mk 2 Sea Kings. A total of 11 aircraft have been delivered to the RAN, the first 10 numbered WA787 to WA796. The aircraft are normally painted light grey with white tops.

In 1972 Westland projected a land-based troop-carrying version of the Sea King to be dubbed Commando, somewhat cut back to basics with all AS equipment removed, avionics reduced, but with an impressive carrying capacity of 28 fully-armed troops over a 300-mile range and an alternative cargo load of 8,000lb over 150 miles.

The first customer for this version was the Egyptian Air Force which ordered five, designated Commando Mk 1s, or Mk 70s, in September 1973. This order was followed by others for 19 Commando Mk 2s and for six Sea King Mk 47 ASW aircraft. The Commando Mk 1s were externally similar to Sea King Mk 1s with five-bladed tail rotors retained; the Commando Mk 2s had up-rated engines and six-bladed tail rotors, and the Mk 47s were basically similar to the RAN's Mk 50s and RN's Mk 2s.

All the Egyptian aircraft were delivered between 1973 and 1976. Two of the Commando Mk 2s were fitted out with VIP interiors and designated Mk 2Bs.

Above: Australian Mk 50s landing-on. *Westland*

Left: The RAN contract coincided with the production of the 2,000th Gnome engine. *Rolls-Royce*

Right: A MIL Mi-6 general purpose heavy lift helicopter is seen above this Egyptian Commando. *Rolls-Royce*

03
04

Right: Egyptian Air Force technicians during training. *Rolls-Royce*

Below: A Belgian Mk 48. *Rolls-Royce*

At the time of writing a further contract for four Commando Mk 2Es was in prospect. No reliable information on current colour schemes and markings of the Egyptian aircraft was available.

(The Commando concept was later accepted by the RN which preferred to use the designation Sea King Mk 4 for its troop and load carriers partly because the service uses the term Commando Squadron for all its helicopter troop carrying units and confusion could have arisen with such squadrons still using Wessex Mk 5s.)

The Pakistan navy ordered six Mk 45s in December 1972. These were ASW aircraft similar to the RN's Mk 1s but five of them were modified for alternative anti-surface vessel (ASV) operations and made capable of carrying guided missiles. They were shipped out in two batches of three in November 1975 and October 1976. They were painted in dark sea blue with white radomes and bore white side numbers 4510 and 4515 with the word Navy in white. The aircraft were allotted serial numbers WA797 to WA802.

In April 1974 the Belgian Air Force ordered five Mk 48 SAR Sea Kings, basically similar to the German and Norwegian SAR aircraft but with nationally compatible communications radio fits. The Belgian aircraft are painted in green and sand camouflage patterns with red nose and tail sections and bear side numbers RS01 to RS05, with serial numbers WA831 to WA835.

The Gulf state of Qatar became Westland's final customer ordering four Commando Mk 2s (one of them a VIP variant) in January 1974 and later eight Commando Mk 3s, the latter type capable of carrying a wide variety of armaments. The first four Qatar Emiri Air Force Commandos are painted in sand and earth camouflage patterns with pale blue undersides. Serial numbers are WA828, WA829 (the VIP variant), WA 836, and WA837. Black side numbers QA20, QA21, and QA22 are painted on the troop-carrying aircraft.

As a follow-up to the 1966 sales arrangement the RN was given the task of training air and ground crews from most of the customer nations mentioned above. Initially the training arrangements at Culdrose were carried out by ad hoc units named after the customer nations. The dating of the placing of orders did not always follow the same sequence as the delivery of aircraft and the arrival of crews to be trained, and the first in the field were the Indians who were taught on their own aircraft at Culdrose in 1971; the Royal Norwegian Air Force training unit was commissioned in January 1972 and disbanded on completion of its programme the following year.

Right from the start the foreign training units at Culdrose proved that they were not only there for the business of teaching but that they could and would help in live rescue operations thus proving at an early stage the Sea King's enormous SAR potential as well as adding to students' practical experience. On 2 August 1972 a Sea King of the Norwegian training unit was diverted from a training sortie in the Predannack area by a Mayday call to succour the survivors of a Wessex Mk 5 which had crashed near Callington. Lt-Cdr M. F. L. Purse, the unit CO with Capt Saetherbakken RNoAF, took the injured the Stonehouse hospital.

Above: Lt-Cdr David Mallock RN, CO of the Culdrose Foreign Training Unit. *RN*

On 3 October 1972 an aircraft of the unit with a doctor on board flew 20 miles north of Trevose Head to the Russian trawler *Nikelayevski* which had an injured seaman on board. The doctor was winched down to the ship and the injured man taken to Treliske hospital a little puzzled at having been aided by a Norwegian helicopter in the English Channel approaches. Capt Saetherbakken was again aboard together with Lt I. C. Domoney RN and WO Aanensen of the RNoAF.

The Royal Navy Foreign Training Unit was formally commissioned at Culdrose on 12 June 1973 under the command of Lt-Cdr David Mallock RN. Its first clients were the Federal Germany Navy crews with their Sea King Mk 41s. They, Lt-Cdr Mallock and his instructors and air and groundcrews were destined to play a leading role in one of the most dramatic helicopter rescue operations in history and one which was to have a profound effect on the future safety and performance of Sea King aircraft.

Left: Perhaps the most famous Sea King rescue picture ever taken: Culdrose aircraft over the capsized *Merc Enterprise*. Leading Naval Airman (Phot) Steve Collinson took the picture from the door of 'Germany 5'. *RN*

Right: Painting of '92' and 'Germany 5' of the *Merc Enterprise* rescue, by John J. Thomlinson. *RN*

The full story of the *Merc Enterprise* rescue of January 1974 was told in my own book *Helicopter Rescue* (Ian Allan 1980) and earlier in Frank Pearce's *Mayday! Mayday! Mayday!* (Bantam 1977), but certain aspects of it need recalling in a history of the Sea King aircraft. On that morning when hurricane force southwesterlies were blowing down the Channel the 480-ton Danish coaster *Merc Enterprise* capsized south of Plymouth with 16 men and three women aboard. Eleven of the 19 were saved, seven by Culdrose Sea Kings, four by the crew of a Russian trawler. Although at that time there was no formal commitment for RN Sea Kings to participate in civilian rescues they were, of course, always ready to help and when news of the disaster reached Culdrose soon after midday five aircraft went into action. Two of them, Nos 592 and 596, came from No 706 Squadron, by then the Advanced Sea King Training Unit at Culdrose; one, 051, from No 824 Squadron, and two German-owned aircraft from the FTU which adopted callsigns 'Germany 5' and 'Germany 7' — the last being already airborne and dealing with a false alarm Mayday call off Land's End.

In this particular narrative it is the performance of 'Germany 5', full side number 89-55, which deserves study. This aircraft was commanded by Lt-Cdr Mallock himself. His second pilot was Kapitanleutnant Otto Reiners, aged 29, FGN; his Observer was Lt Alan Tremelling RN and his winchman Leutnant Max Schueler FGN. LNA (Phot) Steve Collinson had also jumped aboard to take pictures and do anything else he could to help.

At the scene Max Schueler lifted two live survivors and two dead bodies from the sea in spite of injuries and damage to his immersion suit inflicted by a panicking survivor. 'Germany 5' headed for the helicopter pad at HMS *Drake*, the Plymouth shore base, a difficult journey for all on board because the Master of *Merc Enterprise*, Capt Jan Fedderson, was alive and reasonably well but his wife's body lay in the cabin nearly alongside him.

After landing at *Drake*, 'Germany 5' received fresh orders. The skipper of the Russian trawler *Leningrad*, whose crewmen had carried out a great act of gallantry by jumping over the side of their ship into 30ft waves while attached by bowline-knotted ropes,

said over the radio that the ship could not turn across the seas to enter Plymouth Sound and requested a helicopter to lift off his four survivors. David Mallock and the crew of 'Germany 5' attempted just that but had to back off after assessing the size of the seas and the pitch and roll of *Leningrad*. (There are *some* limits even to a Sea King's capability.)

They were given one more job, to look for the Plymouth lifeboat which had broken radio contact off the Eddystone. They found the boat, got reassuring waves from Coxswain John Dare and his crew and thankfully set off Westwards for home at Culdrose, albeit into a 60kt headwind. Then 'it' happened. Various engine surges and power losses developed. At one stage noises akin to those of machine guns firing were heard to the accompaniment of yellow sparks. A speed reduction was made which eased matters a little and two PAN calls (indicating difficulties but not imminent life-and-death danger) were transmitted. Working in fairly finely tuned harmony David Mallock and Otto Reiners finally put 'Germany 5' down in auto-rotation, both engines dead, on a steep sloping field near Porthoustock, cutting a few power cables in the final flare-out, this time to the accompaniment of blue sparks for a change. Meanwhile Sea King '051' had re-scrambled from Culdrose to try to give assistance to 'Germany 5'. Its Captain, Lt Tony Baker, experienced engine surges and power losses as well and made a highly precautionary landing only four miles away from the now downed 'Germany 5'.

It did not take long to work out that both 'Germany 5' and 051 had run into severe salt ingestion problems and much was to be learned from their experiences. Both aircraft, out of sheer necessity, had been hovering (or 'loitering') for several hours at low altitude over 30ft and more waves with salt-laden spray flying to at least 500ft. It had done no good to the turbine blades of the otherwise faithful Gnomes. The engines of both aircraft were sent all the way back to Rolls-Royce at Leavesden where serious long-term corrosion of turbine blades was identified.

The near loss of two aircraft and the people aboard them led to *no* recriminations, only to a careful constructive examination of the problem, the results of which have not eliminated it, but at least put it under control.

It has turned out that so far there is no short-term and complete answer to the problem of salt ingestion into the engines of helicopters which *have* to fly for most of their lives at low levels over the sea, and which in order to do their jobs have to do just that in foul weather as well as fine.

The 'barn door' FOD (Foreign Object Damage) shield for Sea Kings which Sikorsky's had evolved before the *Merc Enterprise* epic provides only a partial answer. The 'barn door' to be seen mounted on most Sea Kings from 1974 onwards was really designed to prevent the ingestion of ice or other solid objects. As most schoolboys know, ice and salt do not normally go together. What was learned from the experiences of David Mallock and Tony Baker was the need to appreciate the problem, to identify the symptoms, and take corrective action.

Various options are open to a helicopter captain who suspects his engines are being subjected to salt ingestion. (Few of them *were* open to David Mallock and Tony Baker at the time of the *Merc* rescue because their only concern was to go on trying to save lives.) He can, if he is lucky, find a friendly cloud, break off from his job, and give his engines a fresh water shower in it. Alternatively, having assessed the risk, and perhaps noticed power loss, break off from the job altogether and land to have his engines washed out by maintainers using compressor hoses and fresh water with perhaps something like 'Daz' added.

A more drastic solution was put forward at one stage to equip Sea Kings with an in-flight Turco-dust cleansing device. Turco-dust consists of a mixture of chemical particles reinforced (amazingly) by ground-up apricot shells. It is an excellent cleansing agent for fouled-up turbine blades but is rather like the scouring powder Mum used to clean her saucepans and understandably is viewed with some suspicion by many maintainers, especially since it can get into some unwanted places in the total mechanism of a helicopter. FAA maintainers and RAF ground crews are prepared to use it, but with caution.

The long term lessons that were learned from the *Merc Enterprise* experience were those which pointed to the training of pilots to be aware of the problem, to

Above: The effect of salt water ingestion on a turbine wheel. This Rolls-Royce photograph was taken after a 345hr sortie pattern endurance test simulating ingestion. Blade material was changed with the introduction of the H1400-1 Gnome engine due to the need for improved 'creep resistance'.

Left: A Mk 2 Sea King with 'unmodified' barn door Foreign Object Damage shield fitted. *Rolls-Royce*

Right: A Mk 5 Sea King with modified barn door FOD shield. The aircraft is actually making an emergency soft-belly landing on to mattresses because of a damaged undercarriage sponson. *RN*

recognise it, and take appropriate action in good time. That they were lessons well learned was proved during the Falklands conflict when Sea Kings and other helicopters were flying almost constantly in maximum risk salt ingestion conditions, yet none succumbed to that particular hazard, among all the others that were present.

The Foreign Training Unit at Culdrose was involved in another rescue operation of great significance in January 1975 when yet another coaster, the British-registered MV *Lovat*, capsized off Land's End. Two Pakistani-owned Sea Kings, manned by RN crew, were involved in the rescue attempts but because this episode had such a fundamental bearing on the whole use of Sea Kings in the UK SAR structure it will be described in detail in a later chapter. Suffice to say at this stage that the overseas sales of Westland Sea Kings not only brought in some helpful foreign currency but that they materially 'improved the breed'.

A very important asset to all concerned with the Sea King was created in 1970 when the Singer (UK) Link-Miles Flight & Mission Simulator was installed at Culdrose. It contributed to Culdrose being the 'spiritual home' of the Westland Sea King, confirmed it as the main training base not only for foreign customers but also for the RAF SAR organisation. It had up to the time of writing provided more than 40,000 hours of training time (35,000 of them for RN aircrews) at a 98.4% reliability rate. The simulator consists of a pilots' module representing the Sea King cockpit with all controls and instruments mounted on a three-axis moving platform, plus a rear-seat cabin section representing the radar and sonar stations but without motion. Each section has its own control console providing for separate pilots' and 'back-end' sorties, but the two can be joined for full mission crew training. Although the pilots' module is 'blind' with opaque windows, considerable realism can be injected by instructors who can combine malfunctions indicated on the instruments together with unpleasant noises and turbulent movement up to the point of a hard-earth crash.

The simulator has been widely used not only by RN and RAF Sea King crews under initial training and by foreign clients' crews but by others returning for refresher courses. The operating cost is put at about 10% of that of flying 'real' aircraft. For many years it was the only Sea King simulator in Europe although recently it has been matched by others in Germany and elsewhere and by civilian S-61 operators, notably British Airways in Aberdeen. Plans are in hand to replace the present equipment with a fully visual simulator by 1986 and a contract for this was expected to go out in 1984.

Suffice it to say that its present realism was sufficient to produce a considerable output of adrenalin from this author when the instructor took out all stabilisation aids and invited him to hold a Sea King straight-and-level on what is generally termed a razor blade. Guests are, however, usually invited to try this shortly before bar opening time in the Culdrose wardroom and generally recover.

Above: Not actually dive-bombing but putting on a show for Culdrose open day. *Leading Airman (Phot) Pete Northcott/RN*

jolly abbreviation of 'Jumpexes'. The code-name 'Jumpex' comes from the 'Jump' navigation system under which ASW helicopters move from one sonar dunking spot in an ocean to another, working in pairs or larger groups, able to vector each other on to targets, each aircraft capable of killing as well as hunting (the 'ex' means exercise). Much sophistication had also been built up in the 1970s of co-operation with the RAF's long range Nimrod maritime reconnaisance and ASW aircraft, and of course with surface ships bent on the same quest of seeking out and killing submarines. The RN's new breed of aircraft carrier, the 'Invincible' class, was about to come into service, and the Sea Harriers were about to put the FAA back into the front line of aerial warfare. In the Sea King world No 824 Squadron had taken up its new — and to be proved vitally important, deployment — aboard the big ships of the RFA, *Fort Austin* and *Fort Grange*, (23,000 tons) and the 'O' class tankers (18,600 tons).

A Sea King HAS5 of No 810 Naval Air Squadron (in Falkland War colours) operating off RFA *Engadine* in February 1983. *RN*

Some Sea King mothers.

Top: HMS *Invincible* with Harrier and Mk 2 Sea King.
Leading Airman (Phot) Dave Houghton/RN

Above: RFA replenishment ship *Fort Austin* with Sea Kings of No 824 Squadron embarked. *RN*

Right: RFA tanker *Olna*. *RN*

Above: Weapon fit of a Mk 5. *RN*

Below: The weapon fit of a Sea King Mk 5.

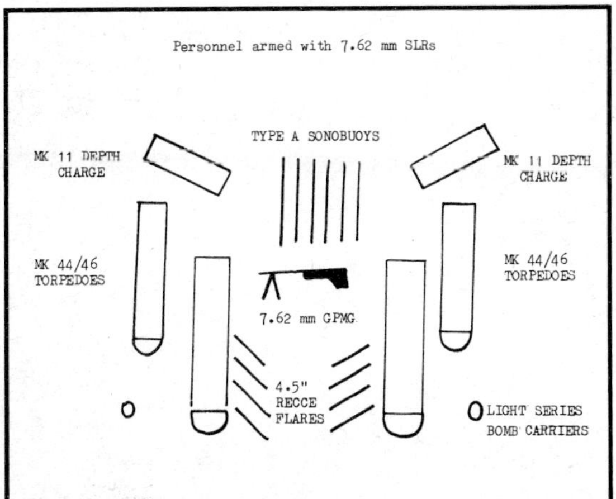

The Sea King is clearly capable of carrying and making use of a vast range of weapons ranging from sponson-mounted machine guns to missiles, including the now notorious Exocet, and several foreign customers have equipped it in this way, but the RN has, overtly at least, preferred to stay with homing torpedoes — Mk 44, Mk 46 and latterly Sting Ray — and/or depth charges.

The Mk 2 to Mk 5 up-grading was considerably more complex than the earlier Mk 1 to Mk 2 process, although there was no major change in engines or gross weight. Development on the Mk 5 began in January 1979, flying started a year later at Yeovil and the first two of the new aircraft were delivered to the Navy in October 1980. Internally the first major change was the introduction of the longer (almost double) range radar, the MEL ARI5991 Sea Searcher. This radar set features a controllable sector width while of course retaining the ability to traverse through a full 360° of scan. It can be set up in three distinctive modes — one in which the helicopter itself appears at the centre of the 17in diameter plan position indicator screen and appears stationary relative to its surround-

072
072

4
704
819 NAVAL AIR SQUAD
04
ROYAL NAVY
DANGER

Above left: The third overseas contract for British-built Sea Kings came from the Royal Norwegian Air Force. The high-visibility paint areas of the colour scheme are most appropriate because they so often have to work in snowy conditions as well as over the sea. *Westland*

Left: Sea Kings are often based aboard ships, so it is important for them to be able to fold their rotors to fit into the limited hangar space available. This HAS2A, XV664/704, of No 819 Naval Air Squadron demonstrates this ability while shore-based at HMS *Gannet*, Prestwick. *Lt Christopher Wood RN*

Above: Egypt ordered six ASW Mk 47s, five Commando Mk 1s and 19 Commando Mk 2s for its armed forces. These are two of the Mk 47s, based on the RN Mk 2s and similar to the Royal Australian Navy's Mk 50s, providing a good view of the open sonar well. *Westland*

Below: A familiar sight on national television screens at the time of the British withdrawal from Beirut in late January 1984 were the RFA *Reliant*-deployed Sea King HC4s of No 846 Squadron, Royal Navy, which played a major part in the airlift. The Union flag-emblazoned aircraft are seen using the Army's airstrip at Dhekelia, Cyprus as a temporary shore base. *Allan Burney*

This picture: A Mk 5 in Falklands war markings. *RN*

General arrangement drawing of the Mk 5 Sea King.

ings; the second with the aircraft appearing to be moving over stationary sea or land; and thirdly in which the helicopter's own position can be offset from the centre of the display.

The dimensions of the Sea Searcher radar called for a redesign of the dome, which came out as the most distinguishable external feature for spotters, looking in shape rather like one of Sir Winston Churchill's favourite forms of headgear instead of resembling an essential part of a steam railway locomotive.

The second and perhaps equally important addition to the Mk 5's ASW equipment was the Marconi LAPADS (Lightweight Acoustic Processing and Display System) which is a major aid in the interpretation of information obtained from passive sonar buoys. LAPADS displays all the required data on a printout chart recorder normally handled by the sonar operator, who in the RN is usually a non-commissioned aircrewman up to the rank of chief petty officer.

Decca 71 Doppler equipment was fitted into the Mk 5s as well as Decca TANS (Tactical Air Navigation System). The latter is essentially a mathematical computer, absorbing inputs from all available navigation sources including gyro-compasses and Doppler, and providing a numerical display which can virtually tell the aircrew where they are (in terms of latitude and longitude, Ordnance grid reference, or Naval Grid), what course to steer on to the next desired point, and advise them when they have reached it.

In the Sea King world the TANS system was first introduced in the RAF's HAR Mk 3s, about which more later in the next chapter. In the RAF aircraft it was mounted in the pilot's cockpit; in the RN's Mk 5s in the Observer's position at the rear — another neat example of the slight difference in service procedure.

An additional launching tube for passive sonar buoys was introduced into the Mk 5 Sea King over and above the arrangement evolved in the No 814 Squadron Jezebel Mk 2s.

Provision was also made for the carrying of another piece of electronic magic called a magnetic anomaly detector, cheerfully abbreviated to MAD. To all intents and purposes MAD is an advanced, and giant-sized version of a mine detector, working on the same basic principles as the device invented by two Polish officers in the 1940s which enabled the Royal Engineers to breach the Alamein minefields. As a confirmatory adjunct to sonar MAD will tell a helicopter captain whether a suspect object is made of metal or whether, after all, it is an innocent whale. The equipment required to use it includes a small torpedo-shaped object on a long wire even more cheerfully named by the Navy the MAD Bird.

Below: A Mk 5 streaming its 'MAD Bird'. *RN*

ROYAL NAVY
DANGER
XV373

Above: The five marks of the Westland Sea King are represented in this unique air-to-air photograph, taken in 1981 while the helicopters were assigned to the A&AEE at Boscombe Down, Wilts. From bottom to top are: HAS1, XV373; HAS2A, XV704; HAR3, XZ587; HU4, ZA293; and HAS5, XZ916. *A&AEE, Boscombe Down*

Below: An excellent view depicting the sort of conditions in which Sea Kings have to perform rescue tasks around Britain's coastline. Interestingly this HAS2A (XV663) has no 'barn door' foreign object deflector in front of the engine intakes. *Westland*

Above: A Mk 1 of No 826 Squadron jettisoning four Mk 44 torpedoes simultaneously off Portland during tests. *RN*

Some changes had to be made to the internal arrangements of the Mk 5 fuselage to accommodate all the new kit. The aft cabin bulkhead was moved back, as had successfully been done in the SAR and Commando modifications, the floor had to be strengthened, and the fuel system of underfloor flexible tanks modified to take care of a backwards shift in the centre of gravity, the LAPADS equipment especially making the helicopter drop its tail rather lower than desirable in the hover.

Again the RN's fleet of Mk 5 Sea Kings was produced by a combination of new-builds from Westlands and conversions at Fleetlands and Culdrose. Between September 1980 and August 1981 Westland produced ZA126 to ZA137, and in 1982 ZA166 to ZA170 (17 new aircraft). Between 1981 and 1982 Fleetlands and Culdrose converted XV647 (from a Mk 2), XV651 (straight from Mk 1), and from Mk 2s XV652, XV655, XV658, XV661, XV675, XV703, XV706, XV709, XV711, XV712 and XV713; XZ571, XZ574 to XZ578, XZ519 and XZ916 to XZ922. Further conversions, and new-builds including replacements for losses sustained during the Falklands conflict, were going on at the time of writing.

The Mk 5 new-build and conversion programme had fortunately become well advanced in time for the RN's unexpected shooting war in the Falklands and these potent aircraft were already part of the complement of the first of the new ships originally called through-deck cruisers, later more simply and sensibly aircraft carriers, HMS *Invincible*, which got to the war in time, and HMS *Illustrious*, which followed hard on *Invincible's* heels. Others were deployed on board the faithful HMS *Hermes*, fortunately reprieved from the scrapyard because of the navy's victory in obtaining its Sea Harriers and needing a training ship to use them from. Others, Mk 5s plus some remaining Mk 2s from 824 Squadron, were on board the RFAs, split into flights of usually two aircraft per ship. More detail of this will be referred to in the chapter entitled 'Sea Kings to War'.

Almost simultaneously with the development work on the Mk 5 Sea King, Westland was called upon by the RN to perfect a version of the 'Commando' to be used as a troop and load carrier and to be designated in RN terms the Sea King Mk 4. This was first flown on 26 September 1979 with the same engines, gearbox and six-bladed tail rotor as the ASW Mk 2, but with

Above: A Mk 4 lifting a Volvo Bandwagen snow vehicle, weighing about 7,500lb. Note 'low response beam' below fuselage which has helped to increase the total underslung load capacity by some 1,500lb.

the stripped-out Commando-type fuselage and no float sponsons (but with emergency flotation bags because the Royal Marine Commandos, the most likely 'passengers', tend to operate from ships and usually have to fly over water to reach their objectives).

The Royal Marine Commandos — especially No 45 which, thankfully in the light of the Falklands war, spend a great deal of their time training in Arctic terrain — particularly welcomed some Mk 4 Sea Kings for their annual 'Clockwork' exercise in Norway during the winter of 1979-80.

Westland was able to deliver a batch of Mk 4s in November 1979 and the Navy was able to test and demonstrate their enormous lifting capability and their reliability in hostile climatic conditions. Among other things it was proved that they could lift, in one go, a two-part Volvo snow vehicle, approaching 8,000lb, as an underslung load. The Volvo, sometimes erroneously referred to as a Sno-Cat, is the mainstay of all British Army operations on the Northern Flank of NATO and the previously available Wessex helicopters could only move one in two parts. Since the Volvo is not much use unless its two ends (each using power-driven rubber tracks) are joined together, some embarrassment to the military can be caused if the halves are deposited at any great distance from one another. The underslung load lifting capacity of all Sea Kings, especially Mk 4s, is enhanced by a piece of equipment called a 'low response beam' which adjusts the aircraft's centre of gravity and prevents a heavy weight underneath the aircraft from oscillating back and forth and thereby causing problems to the pilot trying to maintain fore-and-aft trim with his cyclic stick, albeit with all sorts of aids from Louis Newmark and others.

Thirty Mk 4 Sea Kings were ordered by the Navy in September 1978 and No 846 (Commando) Squadron was fortunately fully equipped and experienced with them by the time of the outbreak of the Falklands war. At the time of writing another 'squadron's worth' was in course of production and delivery plus replacements for those lost during the latter conflict. In their usually cheerful and self-deprecating manner air and ground-crews of the Navy's Commando squadrons ('Junglies' as opposed to the 'Pingers' of the ASW squadrons) refer to the Mk 4 as a 'flying lorry', but their respect for it, and that of others, should become clear later.

RAF
RESCUE
XZ598
RESCUE

W
NAVY
G-17-15
DANGER
IN510
WESTLAND
HELICOPTERS

Left: One of the first roles anticipated for helicopters was the rescue of ditched aircrew. This Royal Air Force Sea King HAR3, XZ598, of No 202 Squadron, is seen operating over the Northumbrian coast from RAF Boulmer.
Peter Scott, Rolls-Royce

Below left: Almost identical to the RN Sea King Mk 1, an Indian Navy ASW Mk 42 over Westland Helicopters' factory at Yeovil. *Westland*

Right: A Belgian Mk 48 carrying out a routine double-lift rescue exercise — note the downwash effect on the sea surface below the helicopter. The Mk 48 is a Search and Rescue variant similar to the West German and Norwegian aircraft, each having nationally compatible radio fits.
Westland

Below: A Royal Navy Sea King HAS2 about to touch down at RNAS Culdrose, Cornwall. *Peter Scott, Rolls-Royce*

The Safety Record

Twenty-six Sea Kings of the RN had ditched or crashed up to the time of writing over a 13-year period of the aircraft type service. 14 of these aircraft were recovered and repaired. 12 aircrew were killed in the accidents, plus 21 passengers in the 'great disaster' — the loss of No 846 Squadron's Mk 4 'Victor Tango' during the Falklands war. One RAF crewman was killed in a SAR incident. It was known that the Germans and the Norwegians had each lost a Westland-built Sea King; and one other RN aircraft, Mk 4 ZA290, was deliberately burned by its crew during an incident in the Falklands War. As recorded earlier one of the first development aircraft (XV372) was written-off in 1969, making a total of 30 serious accidents among some 250 aircraft built.

The accident record, particularly that affecting the RN's aircraft, must be put into perspective by assessing the hazards of ASW flying, even with the best equipment available in the world and the highest standards of skills and disciplines obtainable. The safety record of the basic aircraft type must also be measured against the statistics of operators using the civilian S-61 versions in hostile weather and over the frequently hostile North Sea in the oilfield operations. These (involving British, Dutch and Norwegian operators) amount to a total of eight serious accidents, six aircraft lost and 40 people killed, during a 10-year period of about 1,700 annual flying hours, many of them in extreme weather conditions. It would be about as stupid for anyone to brand the S-61 design as a dangerous one as it was to give a similar label to the DC3/Dakota in the late 1940s and 1950s when there were precious few other types of commercial aircraft flying anywhere in the world.

Below: This picture, taken by Capt Campbell Bosanquet of British Airways Helicopters, illustrates the weather conditions frequently encountered in the North Sea. It shows the *Treasure Finder* semi-submersible accommodation rig in the Brent Field in a wind strength of 68kt gusting to 78kt. Similar conditions are of course encountered by service and civilian rescue helicopters but it is seldom anyone has time to photograph them. Capt Bosanquet took the picture from the flightdeck of another S-61 waiting to land on.

Left: The civilian versions of the Sikorsky-built S-61s have played a major part in rescue tasks over the North Sea oilfields, in the ownership of British Airways Helicopters, Bristow, and some other private operators. This picture shows a Bristow S-61 carrying out a typical rescue exercise with an RNLI lifeboat. *Bristow Helicopters*

Below: A Mk 5 dunking. *RN*

An aerial frigate. The RN uses the Sea King as a submarine hunter-killer — its manoeuvrability and speed is much greater than that of any ship, yet it can carry an impressive array of weapons and equipment. This is an HAS5 of the newly-formed No 810 NAS, sonar dipping on exercise. *RN*

The main hazard to ASW Sea King crews is the absolute necessity to hover low over sometimes enormous seas, often in darkness, in order to carry out the job which they, and the aircraft, are all about. The standard sonar dunking altitude is 40ft. (Waves of 30ft are common in heavy weather in northern latitudes. Those of 40ft and much more are perhaps infrequent but by no means exceptional). During such procedures the slightest 'hiccup' — perhaps in an engine or its computer-controlling mechanism, perhaps in the usually faithful automatic flying control system, perhaps in the Human Brain Mk 1 — can put a Sea King into the water, and by all the laws of aviation, including that of the often-quoted 'Sod', it will usually be very rough, very cold, water. Even with its two potent and reliable Gnome engines, a Sea King 'dunking' with anything like a full fuel load aboard and perhaps armed with a mixture of torpedoes and depth charges, is seldom 'safe single engine'. The capsizing problem will remain until there can be fundamental rethinking about helicopter design and the placing of centre of gravity.

There have, of course, been disasters which should not have happened, such as that on 21 March 1974 when XV702 from No 824 Squadron flew into a cliff on return from a night dunking exercise in Falmouth Bay, and when XZ917 and XZ915 exercising from HMS *Invincible* south of the Isle of Wight collided in midair with five of the eight aboard them both, killed outright.

The substantial number of survivals from such incidents as ditching due to engine malfunction at low level, loss of tail rotor control or sheer human error remain a tribute to the high standard of escape drills and to the physical fitness of all concerned. Escape from a capsized Sea King, or from any other type of helicopter for that matter, is not all that far from getting out of a submarine. The crew have to wait, while upside down, disorientated, and in total darkness for a number of very long seconds until the rotor blades have ceased thrashing through the water and therefore ceased to be capable of thrashing straight through anyone unwise enough to get in their way. Then they have to feel their way to appropriate escape hatches (having remembered how to undo their harnesses upside-down in the dark), restrain themselves from inflating their life-jackets too soon, remember how to open the hatches having reached them, and finally swim several strokes underwater before surfacing and getting on with the rather cosier business of getting into life rafts, initiating their beacons and settling down with seasickness pills until hopefully another helicopter dangles a rescue strop in front of them, or some sort of boat comes alongside.

The other hazards affecting all naval helicopters are of course concerned with the landing on to, and taking off from, heaving and rolling decks. There are many, very complicated, limits set on both procedures, impossible to detail in a book of this sort. Obviously the centre of the flight deck of a carrier like *Invincible* or *Hermes* will present fewer problems than the stern end 'spot' of an RFA tanker in heavy weather. Remarkably few accidents have been recorded from this form of hazard, however, at least for public consumption. ('Haul down' gear is available for Sea Kings to assist in the matter of deck landings but for a number of reasons has not found favour with the Royal Navy.)

Below left: Sea King XV667 of No 826 Squadron then embarked in HMS *Tiger* ditches in a heavy sea (State Six) and remains upright long enough for the crew to escape and board their dinghy.

Below: Approximately 30 seconds later. This photograph proved the cause of the 'severe vibrations' which led to the ditching. The rotor blade lying in the forward position is several feet shorter than it should have been.

Above and below: Copy book stuff. XV703 'sitting like a duck' alongside HMS *Hermes*. The aircraft was recovered undamaged. *RN*

Above and left: The one that got ashore. '142' on Swanpool Beach . . . and being taken home to Culdrose with the help of the USAF.
Both: LA (Phot) Chris North/RN

Below: This British Airways S-61N had to make an emergency water alighting 18 miles off Aberdeen in July 1980 whilst inward bound from an oil rig. Crew and passengers took to their dinghy from which they were speedily rescued by other helicopters and ships. The aircraft was towed in to port by the Aberdeen lifeboat and hoisted ashore by dockyard crane.
J. D. Ferguson, Aberdeen RNLI

Above: 'Tugg' Willson's view of 142's adventure, as portrayed in *Cockpit*, the Royal Navy Flight Safety magazine. The artist, a retired Fleet Air Arm Officer, has made a notable contribution to flight safety through his 'in-humour' portrayals of things that can, and do, happen.

Below: This BA S-61N suffered a gearbox problem in March 1983 while inward bound to Aberdeen. Note airbags deployed on the sponsons. All 17 occupants were winched to safety by an RAF Sea King from Lossiemouth. *No 120 Squadron RAF, Kinloss*

The crew inflated the flotation bags and Lt Wells found that by applying gentle power to his main rotor with the remaining engine he was water-taxying at about 5kt. His Mayday call brought a safety boat, another Sea King and an RNLI inshore lifeboat to the area and all three acted as escorts as 42 began a long, steady voyage towards land with a glistening bow-wave admired by all. Coastguard headquarters suggested Swanpool Beach, just southwest of Falmouth, as a suitable haven and one hour and 50min from touch-down 42 waddled ashore up a gentle slope like a very large and a very noisy duck. After removal of the rotor blades it was airlifted back to Culdrose virtually undamaged by an American Super Jolly Green Giant from Woodbridge. Lt Wells received a commendation from Rear-Adm 'Ted' Anson (the Flag Officer Naval Air Command), who pointed out that no one would have questioned the decision if the aircraft captain had decided to abandon ship.

The incident proved that given a fair chance Sea Kings *will* stay upright on water. The civilian S-61s, with their larger float sponsons in fact stand a better chance and there have been several occasions when they have done so during the North Sea oil operations. Civilian companies train their crews in water alighting and taxying but have to set aside spare aircraft for the task because of corrosion possibilities. The RN and the RAF prefer to train their crews in the art theoretically and 42's exploit is used as a standard lesson on the subject.

Below: A Bristow S-61N being used for water landing and taxying training on the Loch of Skene. Egress from the civilian S61s for passengers in the event of a ditching is considerably easier than that for the crew of a 'bombed-up' ASW Sea King. Sikorsky claims that civilian S-61s should stay upright in seas of up to 'State 7' — near gale conditions. This was of no avail in the British Airways S-61 disaster off Scilly in July 1983 when 'Oscar November' struck the sea at a shallow angle and fairly high forward speed, with one of the undercarriage sponsons ripped off by the impact. *J. D. Ferguson*

Sea Kings to the Rescue

Above: A BA S-61N with rescue strop lowered from its detachable winch. In many rescue situations the location of the cargo door forward and with winch operator close behind the pilots, offers advantages over the military S-61 versions in which the winching position is about 20ft further aft. This picture was taken during an exercise with Aberdeen University's RN Unit ship, HMS *Thornham.* Note position of the radome — a standard arrangement on most civilian versions of the S-61. *J. D. Ferguson*

By the mid-1960s helicopters had established themselves as having a vital role to play in this nation's provisions for the saving and preservation of life both at sea and on land, with six RAF and three RN 'declared' rescue flights dotted around the UK coastline. All these units were equipped with Whirlwinds which had by then earned a magnificent reputation for reliability, quick reaction and general sturdiness, but towards the end of the decade the requirement became clear for longer range aircraft, with twin-engine safety, and particularly for helicopters which could operate in darkness and in all but impossible weather conditions.

Some of the lobbying for a re-equipment programme came from within the RAF which was beginning to push its own interceptor fighters further and further across the North Sea and beyond to exercise and to keep track of Soviet reconnaissance aircraft. Some came from the Scottish fishing industry, some from the then embryo North Sea oil industry.

Ironically West Germany and Norway were already in process of purchasing their own British-built Westland Sea Kings specifically for rescue purposes and the crews were being trained by the RN. Other Scandinavian countries were equipping themselves with other types of long range rescue helicopters including American-built S-61s. The RN had already proved the potential of the Sea King as a rescuer even during its early trials and its aircraft were available to help civilians in distress, but only on an ad hoc basis if and when they were in the right place at the right time.

An interim forward move was made in 1971 when the then Department of Trade & Industry, through its Coastguard branch, funded a contract under which at least one Aberdeen-based S-61N of British European Airways Helicopters Ltd would be on a maximum one-hour reaction time for rescue work. The aircraft were part of the company's fleet of passenger carriers, mainly employed on oil rig services, but detachable winches and other items of rescue equipment were held in readiness at Dyce (Aberdeen) and at Sumburgh (Shetland). A small team of winchmen winch operators was recruited, most of them with previous SAR experience in the RN or the RAF, and a high proportion of BEA (later BA) helicopter pilots voluntarily underwent SAR training, a number of aircraft captains learning the techniques of winch operating and of being winchmen on the end of the wire. This organisation achieved remarkable results, lifting nearly 200 people in distress in the first seven years of its existence. Reaction times were reduced from the statutory hour to something nearer 10 or 15 minutes on most occasions in spite of the necessity to fit a Lucas Aerospace detachable winch in quick time to the nearest available S-61 'bus'. Until its headquarters was moved from Aberdeen to Sumburgh to keep up with the northward march of the oil platforms it provided a unique 'flying intensive care unit', under which an S-61 could take a doctor aboard and be fitted in short time with specially designed surgical and medical equipment, to which many a grievously injured seaman or fisherman owed his life on a long haul back against a headwind after an accident in the middle of the North Sea.

In December 1977 the crew of an S-61 from Sumburgh carried out one of the 'great helicopter rescues' — that of the skipper and crew of the Aberdeen trawler *Elinor Viking*, aground at night on the notorious Ve Skerries reef northwest of Papa Stour, Shetland, and being pounded to pieces by a Force 9 to 10 storm. All aboard were saved and the event has entered the growing folklore of helicopter rescues.

The Shetland Dot rescue contract has now been taken over by Bristow Helicopters Ltd, using an S-61 with special SAR equipment.

On the Saturday morning of 25 January 1975 one of those all too frequent maritime disasters occurred in the Western Approaches which proved beyond all doubt the case of the protagonists for the formalised Sea King rescue service in the UK. The 1,000ton London registered coaster *Lovat*, punching into a Force 8 southwesterly 25 miles off Land's End, suffered a shift of its cargo of fine coal, became in imminent danger of capsize, and the Master, Capt Leslie Beeson, put out a Mayday at 06.22hrs. The nearest 'declared' helicopter rescue facility was the Whirlwind SAR Flight at RNAS Culdrose, officially limited to daylight flying. Land's End Coastguard informed the Culdrose duty officer of the *Lovat's* situation at 06.53hrs. First light, or 'civil twilight' on that day was 07.29hrs.

The Whirlwind scrambled at 07.43hrs after a 14min delay caused by difficulty in establishing air-to-ground radio communications. It was by then assessed that with the best efforts in the world the Whirlwind would only be able to lift three possible survivors out of a known crew of 13 when fuel consumption, distance, hovering time and headwinds were taken into account. Immediate steps were therefore taken at Culdrose to scramble a Sea King. In spite of it being on a Saturday morning with most who would be concerned rightfully in bed at home, one lifted off at 08.50hrs just 90 minutes from the time it was called for by the duty Lieutenant-Commander Flying.

The aircraft was in fact the property of the Pakistan Navy but was crewed by RN staff of the Foreign Training Unit and from No 706 Squadron, the second pilot being Lt Hugh Clark who seven years later in the Falklands was to play a leading part in one of the most publicised helicopter rescues in history. Using the callsign 'Papa 3' they arrived on scene to find the *Lovat* had foundered and that the Whirlwind, piloted by Lt Marsh RN, had run into serious difficulties. Leading Aircrewman LACMN Peter Gibbs had gone down on the wire to a liferaft which had five men and a boy aboard with others in the water nearby. He was first pushed under the water by a man he had tried to help into the strop and had to be winched back up by his fellow crewman, LACMN Paul Mansell. On his second descent the Whirlwind lurched heavily in turbulence caused by the well-meaning efforts of a ship trying to provide a lee, and the winch wire wrapped itself round his throat. LACMN Mansell had no option but to cut the wire with the explosive device provided on all rescue helicopters for such eventualities. After extricating himself LACMN Gibbs swam to the liferaft, boarded it and dragged a seaman in with him. By this time Lt Marsh reluctantly had to turn back to land because of fuel shortage and an unusable winch.

By the time Sea King 'Papa 3' arrived overhead three of the occupants were dead but two were lifted alive as well as three bodies and, finally LACMN Gibbs. Surgeon Capt Boyle RN who was aboard the Sea King was able to give immediate first aid to the two survivors, both of whom were suffering from severe hypothermia. A second Pakistani Sea King with an RN crew reached the area soon after but no further survivors were found alive. The remaining bodies were recovered by the Penlee lifeboat and the minehunter HMS *Wilton*.

Left: Leading Naval Aircrewman Peter Gibbs QGM, shortly after the *Lovat* incident. Peter Gibbs, now a PO Aircrewman, is still serving in the Navy's SAR organisation. *RN*

mark. The whole arrangement was designed to suit administrative convenience at Culdrose, a station which with its Sea King simulator, a vast store of experience on the type and maintenance back-up had by then become the 'university' for anyone about to operate the aircraft type.

The Navy as usual tried to inject some amusement into any threat of an unseemly brawl by producing a document called *The Idiot's Guide to Naval Terminology.* It included such essential items as the signal 'RPC', meaning 'Request the Pleasure of your Company' or more earthily for their guests: 'You are invited to a booze-up'; 'Adrift' meaning 'Late'; 'SPLOT' meaning 'Senior Pilot'; and 'Boat' meaning a ship's boat or a submarine but *not and never* a ship. Many additions were made and eventually it ran to six closely typed foolscap pages.

Left: Six RAF SAR Sea Kings will probably never again be photographed together in the air unless the nation's SAR coverage is suddenly abandoned. *Leading WREN Photographer S. Hill/RN*

Below: The rescue helicopter 'with the mostest'. XZ598 of 'A' Flight, No 202 Squadron, Boulmer carrying out a double-lift winching demonstration. *Peter Scott, Rolls-Royce*

Left: Some of the craggier parts of the Northumberland coast are ideal for winchman training. One of the problems for a rescue winchman on 200ft or more of wire is 'spinning', and this one has his right hand extended in order to prevent it happening. *Rolls-Royce*

Bottom left: An asset which helicopters do possess is the facility for ground crews to cure undercarriage malfunctions *before* an expensive and possibly painful belly landing has to be made. *Westland*

When the RAF completed the conversion of its first Sea King SAR crews the SKTU was wound down to a two-aircraft unit under the umbrella of No 706 NAS, the permanently resident advanced aircrew training unit at Culdrose, and eventually to an independent RAF unit, residing at the station in order to use the simulator and other back-up facilities while providing continuation and refresher training on the aircraft type.

The Westland Mk 3 Sea Kings supplied to the RAF were the last word in helicopter rescue technology. They were powered by the up-rated Gnome 1400-1 engines and had everything going in the way of avionics aboard including the Decca TANS system in the cockpit which was to prove of enormous value in difficult rescue operations. Radio communication equipment included homing facilities on the UHF (Sylvania ARC607) and VHF (Sylvania ARC115) sets. Like the Navy's Sea Kings they had long range HF radio (Collins 618T) and homing facilities to take them on to ditched pilot's rescue beacons, initially SARBRE, later to be replaced by more advanced types.

As with other RAF and Navy rescue helicopters there were initial difficulties in arranging direct RT communications with police and volunteer ground rescue organisations, particularly when engaged in mountain rescue tasks. This problem, by the time of writing, had been almost overcome by the installation of Pye Olympic VHF sets compatible on frequency channels with those used by most ground emergency organisations except the police. Up to the end of 1983 the Home Office still steadfastly refused to allow anyone to use a police radio on a police frequency apart from a policeman. For the rescue Sea King crews the matter was still further compounded because police radios operate Duplex — the caller transmitting on one frequency and the respondent on another. This remained an irritation in some rescue situations but not much more than that. It was always possible to take a policeman aboard with his radio or, better, leave an RAF portable radio with the policemen on the ground.

Like most of the RN's Sea Kings they carried the MEL lightweight radar, Decca Type 71 Doppler, Decca Mk 19 Navigator, Decca 671 VOR/ILS, Decca AVQ75 distance measuring equipment, Marconi AD370S automatic direction finder, and of course, the now faithful Smiths APN198 radar altimeter.

The RAF's Mk 3s had their fuselage cabin bulkhead extended rearwards as in the case of the earlier German and Norwegian SAR aircraft giving accommodation for a notional 18-20 survivors. Radius of action and lifting capabilities of rescue helicopters are impossible to quantify in simple terms because all the calculations depend upon fuel load required to carry out the outward and inward flight, the 'loitering time' (at maximum fuel expenditure) required to lift survivors, and headwind strengths. A very average capability of the RAF's Sea Kings is, however, a 250nm 'out-and-back' range with 12 survivors aboard.

The Sea Kings allocated to the RAF bore the serial numbers XZ585 to XZ599. No ZA105 came in as something of an afterthought but XZ587 was diverted to Boscombe Down for special trials leaving No 202 Squadron and the Training Unit at Culdrose with 15 aircraft in 1983.

When the Mk 3 Sea Kings were first introduced into the RAF's SAR service some doubts were expressed, particularly by experts in the difficult art of mountain rescue, about them possibly being too big, too unwieldy, and liable to create too much downdraught for them to be as effective as the Whirlwinds and Wessex during inland rescue operations. Undoubtedly the downdraught from any large and heavy helicopter can cause problems in rescue situations. Over the sea a Sea King, with all-up weight approaching 10 tons, will kick up the equivalent of a 50kt (strong gale or Force 9) wind on the periphery of its downwash circle. This can be uncomfortable for an unfit and short-winded survivor especially as the effect is to produce very nasty little short waves (about 2ft high and 12in apart) which fill the survivor's mouth with sea every time he opens it to gasp in some air. (The author writes about this problem with feeling, having experienced the sensation while being 'wet-winched' at night from a Sea King under exercise conditions.) Over land, especially during a mountain rescue operation, the downwash from a Sea King can blow away tents and other ground survival equipment, and could possibly dislodge the hand hold of a rescuee clinging to a rock edge (though this has never happened). Most of the potential downwash problems have solved themselves because of the Sea King's possession of a long winch wire — extended by the 1980s to 245ft — and the ability of crews to use it, in spite of 'spinning' risks, enabling rescues to be carried out at relatively high altitude. It has also been found that much of the downwash effect of a heavy helicopter operating in mountains is naturally dispersed by ridges and crags.

Any doubts about the ability of the Sea King to carry out rescues in mountains were finally dispelled in a report submitted by Flt Lt Bob King, an RAF QHI (Qualified Helicopter Instructor) in October 1978, after he and two other experienced pilots had carried out exhaustive trials in the Cairngorms, the Grampians, and the Cullin Hills of Skye. His report concluded:

'The Sea King is a good helicopter for mountain operations and provides a stable working platform.

'It should cope with most weathers and with careful handling and consideration can offer a high degree of safety.

Left: Links between the helicopter rescue service and the Royal National Lifeboat Institution are now very close on a 'mutual respect' basis. A symbolic picture by *J. D. Ferguson*

'The downwash problem in the hills has shown itself not to be excessive and can be further reduced with careful handling. However it would be wrong to completely minimise or even forget that a problem can exist.'

Many operational SAR crews from the RN and the RAF have proved Flt Lt King's assessment 'for real' since he made it in 1978 up to the present day, and even the most suspicious of the ground mountain rescue teams now accept that the Sea King is an ever present help in time of trouble in their terrain. Most of the deeds of the Navy's and the RAF's Sea Kings in the rescue world over the past eight years or so have been well recorded. On a very rough average about 300 *civilians* every year owe their lives to British Sea King helicopters and more importantly, to the crews who man them. So do a great many members of the British and US armed forces.

Details of some of the more recent deeds earn a place in any book about the Sea King helicopter. On 27 March 1980 the hotel rig *Alexander L. Kielland* in the North Sea Ekofisk oil field, about midway between Teesside and Stavanger, put out a Mayday call at 18.29hrs because the whole vast structure with hundreds of people aboard was listing heavily in 60kt winds accompanied by 30ft waves and was about to capsize. The subsequent rescue operation, at least in its early stages, was almost exclusively a helicopter affair, with Sea Kings in the forefront.

From the British side an HAR3 of 'A' Flight 202 Squadron RAF scrambled from Boulmer 10 minutes after the first Mayday, using callsign 'Rescue 31'. It was crewed by Flt Lt Robert Neville (P1), Flt Lt Michael Lakey (P2), FS John Moody (Navigator and winch operator) and FS Michael Yarwood (Winchman). They reached the designated search area by 20.30hrs and 90 minutes later saw a rescue raft with 10 people aboard. FS Yarwood descended to help survivors into this aircraft's rescue strop and in the course of the operation had to drop into the sea twice himself and then clamber aboard the liferaft. The crew of 'Rescue 31' then dropped these survivors on to the nearest oil rig, ascended to 2,000ft to clear gathering fog and generally 'have a think'. Almost immediately they picked up a bleep signal from an automatic beacon. They wound themselves down on to it and saw a lifeboat with 26 people on board. FS Yarwood made yet another winch wire descent to examine the conditions on board the boat, declared they were not absolutely critical and recommended to his aircraft captain that they should mark the position and guide surface rescue vessels to it. Meanwhile, Norwegian SAR Sea Kings from No 330 Squadron RNoAF based at Sola near Stavanger were also in action and winched up 43 survivors from two liferafts. One of them, callsign 'Viking 50', picked up 30 people, Capt Oyvind Ottesen in command, with Airman First Class Wilfred Ramstad down on the wire. At one stage a liferaft became entangled in 'Viking 50s' winch wire and Airman Ramstad had to dive into the sea to cut it. 'Viking 51' (Capt Nils-Reidar Roaldsay), another Westland-built Sea King lifted 13 survivors from a liferaft.

Wind and seas were high throughout the night and visibility low, calling for the full use of all the avionic equipment aboard the RAF and RNoAF Sea Kings. At one stage the 'On Scene Commander', the captain of an RAF Nimrod, had to restrict the movement of helicopters because of the danger of midair collision, and one near-miss of 70ft was reported. The Norwegians encountered difficulties with their winch gear, one aircraft having to land on a rig and change a frayed wire, another losing its hook. (The RAF encountered winch gear problems during the early days of Sea King operations but these have since been rectified.)

Six months later No 202 Squadron was able to record another 'great' when the Swedish container ship *Finneagle* with 60 tons of dangerous chemicals in its cargo caught fire in a storm 60 miles northwest of the Orkneys on the evening of 1 October. It had 22 souls on board including women and children.

Sea King 'Rescue 37' was scrambled from Lossiemouth together with a British Airways winch-equipped S-61 from Sumburgh. 'Rescue 37' had the ship in sight at 22.30hrs and after messages that the crew and passengers mustered on deck were having difficulty in breathing because of noxious fumes the second stand-by Sea King from Lossiemouth, 'Rescue 38', was also scrambled with an RAF doctor on board. Winching proved extremely difficult for all three helicopters because of the height of the flames from the burning cargo and that of the ship's masts and aerials. While some of the latter were being cut down by the ship's crew 'Rescue 37' and 'Rescue 17' — the BAH S-61 — had to break off their attempts because of fuel shortage and return to Kirkwall Airport on Orkney. 'Rescue 38' was commanded by Flt Lt Michael Lakey who had only just returned to duty at his new posting as Flight Commander at Lossiemouth after having been in London collecting one of several awards for his part in the *Alexander L. Kielland* operation.

(RAF rescue helicopters when in action adopt a series of radio callsigns allocated to each flight. The first aircraft to scramble adopts the lower number, the next the succeeding one, each preceded by the word Rescue. During training, aircraft captains use their own personal callsign numbers preceded by such a phrase as Lossiemouth Helicopter. This gives an immediate indication to Coastguards and other radio users of whether the task in hand is an exercise or for real.) Flt Lt Lakey and his crew eventually winched all aboard the *Finneagle* to safety, using the 'Hi-line' method under which a 100ft rope is first dropped on to the deck of a ship during a low pass more or less vertically overhead. The helicopter is then able to stand off on the ship's port side, clear of masts and other obstructions and with the first pilot in the *right*-hand seat having a reasonably clear view of what is going on at the end of the winch wire. (The command position in a helicopter is, unlike that in fixed-wing aircraft, the right-hand seat because of the now standard layout of main doors and winches on that side.) A ship's crew trained in the Hi-line technique — and most should be by now — then draw the rescue wire in through a parabola and let it back up again via the same sort of route. Sometimes a helicopter winchman goes down on the wire himself to assist on deck; on many occasions this is either unnecessary or impossible. A ship's captain trained in the technique steers about 20° off the prevailing wind to enable the helicopter to hover directly into it and maintain station.

During the *Finneagle* operation there was an obvious danger of a major explosion on board at any time during the 40 minutes it took to complete the winching of 22 people and at one stage a spout of flame from the deck led to a cry of 'Up' from Flt Lt Thomas Campbell, the winch operator, and a very rapid reaction on the collective stick by Flt Lt Lakey. At another point the crew found to their astonishment two women, each clutching a child in her arms had put themselves in the winch-strop together. 'Four for the price of one', Mike Lakey commented later.

Flt Lt Lakey later received the George Medal; Flt Lt Campbell the Air Force Cross; Sgt Richard Bragg, the Winchman, the Air Force Medal; Flt Lt David Simpson (second pilot) the Queen's Commendation for Valuable Service in the Air and Sqn Ldr Hamish Grant, the Senior Medical Officer at RAF Lossiemouth who was aboard voluntarily, the Queen's Commendation for Brave Conduct in the Air.

Many of the Sea King rescue missions from Culdrose and from RN and RFA ships at sea have been well publicised; the work done by No 819 Squadron at HMS *Gannet* (Prestwick), the only permanently shore-based RN ASW Squadron is less well known. Positioned at a point from which it can reach not only the dangerous West Scottish coastline but also the Grampians and other areas beloved of climbers of varying ability, the Squadron has averaged between 40 and 50 rescue sorties a year since becoming a declared SAR unit, on top of its ASW work covering the Clyde Estuary, the Faslane nuclear submarine base, and exercising with NATO vessels.

Of all the rescue operations carried out by a Sea King, that involving 016 of No 820 RNAS on 19 December 1981 received the least public recognition, perhaps because it was an attempt which tragically failed through no one's fault, perhaps because it was overshadowed by other aspects of what became known as the Penlee lifeboat disaster.

When the 1,400ton *Union Star* first reported loss of engine power and possible cargo shift off Wolf Rock, Land's End at about 18.00hrs a Sea King SAR crew consisting of Lt-Cdr Russell Smith (a USN officer on an exchange posting) Lt Stephen Marlow, Sub-Lt Kenneth Doherty and LAC Martin Kennie was sum-

Left: At one stage some doubts were expressed over the Sea King's suitability as a mountain rescue aircraft. No 819 NAS based at Prestwick and No 202 Squadron RAF soon disproved this. Picture shows a No 819 NAS aircraft taking part in an exercise in the Grampians.
Leading Airman (Phot)
Chris North/RN

Above: Aircraft of No 819 Squadron re-enacting in daylight, and as a training SAREX, a rescue from a wreck on the West Scottish coast. These are the conditions which have faced many a Sea King crew but which can seldom be photographed while it is all actually happening, partly because darkness often has to be added to the conditions shown. *RN*

Right: A No 819 NAS aircraft considerately parked on a 'main road' on Skye while collecting a guide for a hill search. *J. D. Ferguson*

Below: For various reasons no pictures were taken relating to the gallant rescue attempt made by the crew of '016' during the *Union Star* and Penlee lifeboat disaster. Exactly three months earlier however, a Sea King of No 706 NAS and the Sennen lifeboat combined to save all 11 crew aboard the capsized Icelandic freighter *Tungufoss* off Land's End. The helicopter crew first winched three men to safety in darkness, then used the floodlights to help the lifeboat rescue another seven, and finally snatched the last crew member off the ship just as it sank beneath him. Both the helicopter and lifeboat crews were awarded the Icelandic Silver Medal. Picture shows from left to right, the naval helicopter crew: Lt Phil Sheldon (see Falklands War chapter) PO Aircrewman J. Collins, Lt Nick Houghton and Lt-Cdr Ray Winchcombe.

moned by bleeper at Culdrose. (The Sea King rescue commitment at Culdrose, on top of that provided by Wessex of the permanent SAR Flight from No 771 Squadron, is met either by the permanently resident No 706 Training Squadron or by a front-line unit temporarily disembarked from its mother ship. On this occasion it was 820's turn for duty.) The aircraft was 'ranged and spread' and the crew mustered in 15 minutes with special SAR equipment loaded including a Pye VHF radio for direct contact with the Coastguard on the Channel 16 maritime distress frequency.

A summary of extracts from Lt-Cdr Smith's formal sortie report tells the story of what followed more graphically than any attempt at descriptive writing.

During transit to the scene a 50kt wind was recorded with 40 to 45ft waves, heavy rain, poor visibility, low cloud and no moon. On arrival overhead of the ship lying beam on to the swell and dragging towards cliffs the wind was recorded as 60-65kt gusting to 75-80kt. At 19.50hrs the crew made their first attempts at normal 'double lift' winch transfers

Above: Sea Kings also often rescue other, lesser, helicopters, even though they sometimes have to be rescued themselves by even bigger ones from the USAF. A RAF Whirlwind in distress being lifted off the beach near Brawdy in Pembrokeshire. *RN*

from the starboard quarter of the ship but the combination of wind velocity, wave height, ship movement and aircraft made this 'impossible' the report said. On the second attempt the winchman came within 15ft of the deck but the aircraft was by then dangerously close to the *Union Star's* mast. Six attempts at a Hi-line transfer were then made. The 100ft line on its own was too short if the aircraft was to be kept at a safe height above the mast so attempts were made to 'extend' it by lowering the winchman on the normal cable first with the Hi-line rope in his hands. During one of these attempts the line caught in the rigging on the mast but was recovered. On one occasion the Hi-line did actually drag across the ship's deck within 3-4ft of members of the crew but no attempt was made to seize it. At another stage a crewman did obtain a hold of the line but the combination of ship and aircraft movement snatched it away again. The idea of knotting two lengths of rope together to make a very high Hi-line was considered but rejected because the spare rope length aboard was too thin. At that stage the wind velocity was recorded as 67-70kt gusting 85kt. At 21.05hrs the aircraft crew estimated there were only 10 minutes left before the ship grounded. They could see the Penlee lifeboat making unsuccessful attempts to get alongside and noted 'there seemed no sense of urgency from the ship's crew'. The ship had however by then swung bows on to the seas so another Hi-line was dropped, but in spite of its 250lb breaking strain it was snapped when the weight on its end was caught by a wave. Two more attempts were made at a 'normal' double lift transfer. 'Swing on winch and ship movement totally unacceptable', Lt-Cdr Smith commented in his report. Between 21.05hrs and 21.25hrs the crew noted that a 60ft high white line of breakers could be seen and that there was no delineation between the cliff tops and the distant horizon. They saw the Penlee lifeboat picked up on to the ship's hatch covers by a wave and slide off backward, saw four people jump into the boat and then saw it striking the ship's side 'a number of times'. The report continued: 'At this point we departed due to the proximity of cliffs/breakers as lifeboat pulled away bows into sea'. After landing back on at Culdrose at 21.35hrs the crew rescrambled at 22.45hrs to search down to a 200ft altitude for signs of survivors. 'Very bad visibility/tubulence, even worse than previously experienced', Lt-Cdr Smith recorded. 'Accurate search flying impossible in the conditions'. (During the whole operation Sub Lt Doherty and LAC Kennie had alternated in the roles of winchman and winch operator. Both had highly perilous moments.) They finally landed back on at Culdrose at 00.22hrs.

Nearly 30 years of rescue work by RN and RAF helicopters, 10 of them in the Sea King era, went unmarred by the accidental loss of a single aircrew or 'client' until the morning of 18 November 1980. On that day a Sea King from 'C' Flight, No 202 Squadron at Coltishall was scrambled after a report that two USAF A-10 Thunderbolts had collided near the Norfolk coast en route to a weapons range. One pilot had ejected safely over land, the other, Lt-Col William Olsen, had attempted to get his damaged aircraft back to his Bentwaters base by flying over the sea and avoiding built-up areas. He lost control a few miles off the coastal village of Winterton and also ejected. The Sea King crew found him with his parachute still partly deployed and being dragged corkscrew-fashion through 15ft waves by a 40-45kt wind. Two of the RAF's most experienced SAR warrant officers, Master Air Electronics Operator John Reeson GM and Master Air Loadmaster Dave Bullock were in the back end. MALM Bullock went down on the wire, was dragged through the sea with Col Olsen and the 3,700lb breaking strain winch cable parted. The rest of the crew, especially Dave Bullock's close friend John Reeson, watched with frustrated helplessness as the pair seemed to become entangled in the parachute lines. The sea was far too rough for a water alighting. A USAF HH-53 Super Jolly Green Giant, already airborne from Woodbridge in response to the first collision alarm, was homed on to the scene and dropped two of its para-rescue crewmen in diving kit. They picked up both men but MALM Bullock and Col Olsen were pronounced dead on arrival in hospital.

The full findings of the inquiry into the tragedy were never published but it is believed that the USAF has now modified its pilots' parachute harnesses and parachute canopies to avert the risk of corkscrewing, the phenomenon thought to have prevented Col Olsen from freeing himself from his harness and making the pick-up a relatively minor routine affair.

The RAF's SAR Sea Kings are shortly to be fitted with secondary, electrically-powered winches but this programme had been recommended before MALM Bullock's death for the good reason that the best made and maintained winches can fail and there would be much frustration for a crew if one did after a long flight through storms or other hazards.

Some discussion was taking place in 1984 towards making the RAF's SAR organisation an 'all Sea King' affair, but there was still a strong lobby in favour of keeping Wessex helicopters in service at bases like Valley, Anglesey and Leuchars, Fifeshire where most of the 'trade' involves short range, very quick reaction sorties.

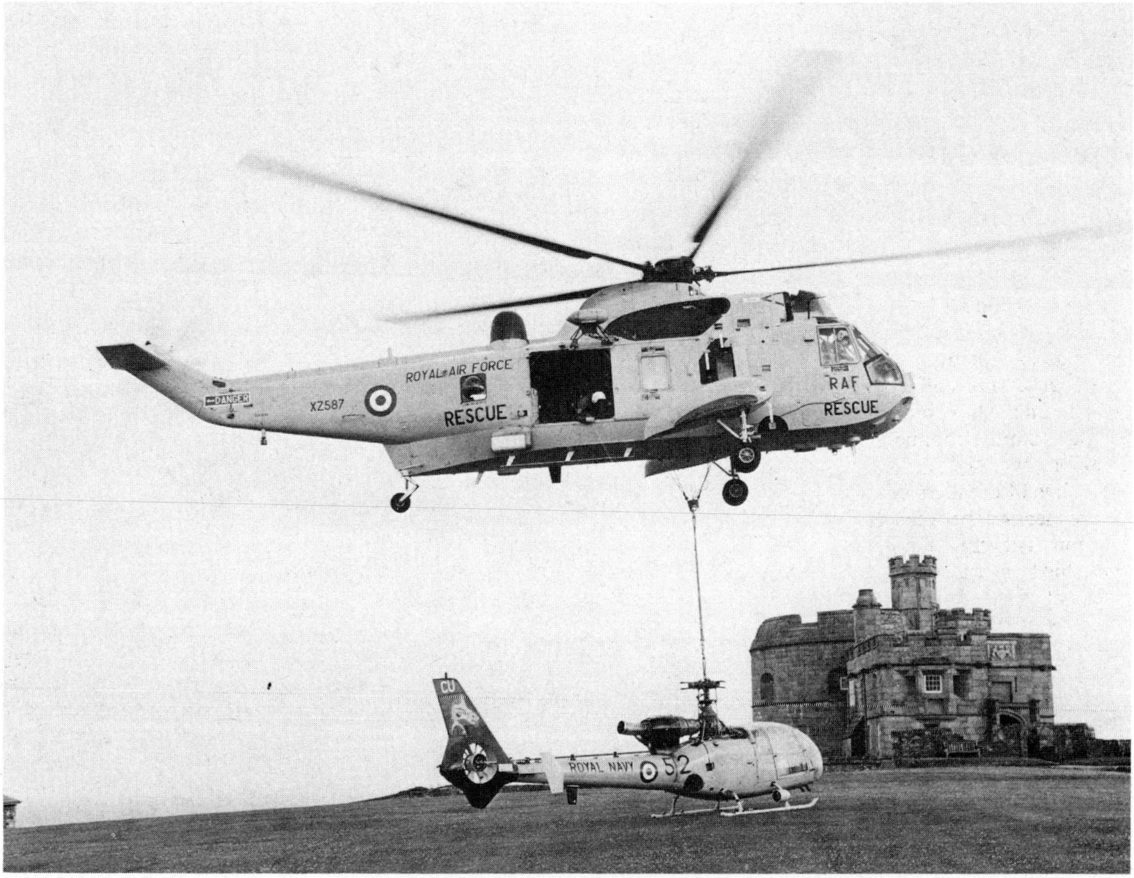

Left: The RAF helps the Army. *RAF*

Above: The RAF helps the Navy.
CPO Paul Yockney/RN

Right: And the Navy helps the Navy.
RN

Sea Kings to War

The Falklands conflict gave Britain its first experience of full-blooded helicopter warfare at sea and all the assessments agree that the fight would not have been won without aircraft of this type in (just about) sufficient numbers, the high quality of them, and the skills of their aircrews and particularly their maintainers. More than 60 Sea Kings of various Marks participated, amassing between them during the months of April, May and June 1982 11,922 flying hours, 5,552 sorties and 8,613 deck-landings. Two Mk 5s and two Mk 4s were lost in accidents, one Mk 4 was burned deliberately by its crew and a Mk 2 was lost in an engine failure ditching in July 1982 after the fighting was over. Prodigious feats of maintenance were carried out, often in the most uncomfortable conditions and commanding officers of all the squadrons involved came back loud in praise of the Sea King's

Above: HMS *Illustrious* with Sea Harriers and Sea Kings ranged on deck. *Westland*

Left: 'Prodigious feats of maintenance were carried out'. Work beginning on a Mk 2 Sea King engine change in the open by maintainers of No 825 NAS.

staunchness and reliability under battle conditions. Aircraft availability rates of up to 90% were claimed with the admission that a certain amount of flying went on under 'exigencies' which might not have been permitted under full peacetime rules. To a large extent this consisted of aircraft being flown if certain equipment not required for the sortie in question was defective. Such bending of the rules was often quite acceptable for the shore-based aircraft employed in troop and load carrying roles during daylight.

The RN's flexible maintenance system which (with certain exceptions) provides for work to be done on an opportunity basis rather than on a rigid periodic arrangement appeared to be well-suited to the conditions encountered. (This system, sometimes looked at askance by RAF engineers, basically stems from sailing ship days when crews varnished the brightwork on fine, calm days, and concentrated on rope-splicing below deck during foul weather.) The proportion of losses to hours flown was not thought in any quarter to be excessive, rather the reverse when the inevitable factor of crew fatigue was taken into account as a contributory cause for some of them.

Weather conditions during most of the campaign were of the kind most disliked by helicopters and their crews — high winds, moisture and salt-laden air, low temperatures hovering on, but usually just above, freezing. Apart from some problems encountered by the shore-based Sea King units from the freezing over of the centre front window of the cockpit, all these were coped with. No serious problems from icing were reported and the obviously high amount of salt ingestion during low flying over stormy seas was kept under control by compressor washing and other precautionary measures.

The RN Sea Kings were operated by No 820 Squadron (Mk 5s) embarked in HMS *Invincible*, No 826 Squadron (Mk 5s) in HMS *Hermes* and RFA *Fort Austin*, No 824 Squadron (Mk 2s) in RFAs *Fort Grange, Olmeda* and elsewhere, No 846 Squadron (Mk 4s) operating from various ships and land bases, and by the specially commissioned and remarkable No 825 Squadron (stripped-out Mk 2s) from land bases and occasionally ships. A detachment of HAR Mk 3s from No 202 Helicopter Rescue Squadron RAF played a significant back-up role at Ascension Island and later moved on to the Falklands soon after the cessation of hostilities.

The task of screening the Fleet against the very real threat of an enemy submarine attack fell mainly on Nos 820 and 826 Squadrons. In April, May and June the first flew 2,150 hours on nearly 700 ASW sorties and nearly as many again on other types of operation including over-sea searches. No 826 Squadron flew more than 3,000 hours. Although it cannot be confirmed that any submarines were detected or attacked the two Squadrons took pride in having achieved their task in that no submarine penetrated nor attacked the Fleet either. A fairly discreet silence was maintained over the expenditure of weapons but as stated earlier it is possible that some whales did come to an untimely end. Both the ASW squadrons were also involved in rescue tasks, one of No 820 Squadron's aircraft performing a particularly difficult one when a Harrier pilot who had ejected into the sea just before last light deliberately switched off his rescue beacon transmitter to avoid detection by Argentinian aircraft. He was found by his small helmet light after several hours of painstaking search pattern flying.

Serviceability averages of between 70% and 80%

Left: 'Weather conditions during most of the campaign were of the kind most disliked by helicopters and their crews'. (These and other pictures of Sea Kings of No 825 Squadron were taken by various unit members under the direction of Lt J. R. Harvey RN, the unit's Photographic Officer.)

Above: Lt-Cdr Ralph Wykes-Sneyd, the CO of No 820 Squadron. *RN*

Above right: A well-known P2 of No 820 Squadron. *RN*

were achieved in both squadrons in spite of the fact that the ASW aircraft had, of course, to be on top line in all respects for both day and night flying. These rates compare with an average of about 60% during peace time flying and speak for themselves of the efforts made by the engineering branch.

Both squadron COs, Lt-Cdrs Ralph Wykes-Sneyd (820) and Doug Squier (826) were awarded Air Force Crosses. No 820 Squadron had no losses, but 826 Squadron lost ZA132 after a single engine failure 'in the dip', and XZ573 after a radar altimeter failure at low level. Both crews were rescued and the latter aircraft in fact had to be sunk by gunfire from HMS *Hermes* because of recovery problems and the operational requirement for the ship not to loiter at the time and place.

No 824 Squadron's aircraft operated in detached flights and carried out a wide variety of tasks from their RFAs including many 'Vertreps', lifting stores between ship and ship and ship to shore, as well as frequently giving ASW cover. This Squadron's CO, Lt-Cdr Ian McKenzie, was awarded the MBE and at one stage took his own three-aircraft flight ashore to operate in the San Carlos bridgehead for four days of non-stop off-loading work from the ships moored there.

No 846 (Commando) Squadron under the command of Lt-Cdr Simon Thornewill (awarded the DSC) flew 3,107 hours on nearly 2,000 sorties in April, May and June with its 11 Mk 4s, rather more than it does in a normal year's training. On the first day of the 're-invasion' seven of its aircraft lifted nearly 1million pounds of stores and equipment and 520 troops. In addition its aircraft played a major part ferrying stores and troops between ships and land during the build-up period at Ascension. In the period 1-18 May, 25 night sorties were carried out over enemy held territory in conditions of low cloud and visibility and strong winds. Only three missions had to be aborted.

Among the ships No 846 Squadron worked from were HMS *Fearless*, and *Hermes*, RFAs *Engadine, Fort Austin* and *Sir Galahad*, and the merchant ships *Canberra, Norland* and *Elk*. Their aircraft played a leading part in the HMS *Coventry and RFA Sir Galahad* rescues.

During the *Coventry* rescue Lt-Cdr Thornewill's own aircrewman, CPO Alf Tupper volunteered to be winched down on to a liferaft, unhooked himself, and swam from raft to raft helping the injured and guiding in waves of rescue helicopters. He was not wearing a survival suit himself but was credited with materially assisting the saving of between 40 and 50 lives. He was awarded the DSM. Later CPO Tupper and his CO were involved in a notable drama when their aircraft, 'Victor Alpha', was bounced by two pairs of Argentinian A-4 Skyhawk jets over land. Fortunately, and unusually, they were flying 'four up' — the Mk 4 Sea King is cleared for single pilot flying providing the aircrewman has been trained in the operation of the emergency manual engine throttles and this system was the rule rather than the exception during the campaign to maximise payloads. On this sortie, however, Lt David Lord RN was in the P2's seat and CPO Tupper, manning a machine gun in the rear door, was accompanied by PO Aircrewman John Sheldon.

Left: Lt-Cdr Ian McKenzie of No 824 Squadron. *RN*

Below: Sea King Mk 4 of No 846 Squadron engaged in a Vertrep.

'Chief' Tupper likens what followed to an improbable sequence from a James Bond film. 'I had my head out of the starboard door and John Sheldon was watching through the bubble window on the left', he recalls:

'Between us we were able to give the management at the front end a pretty interesting running commentary. The CO put the aircraft into a slow left turn first and I cocked the gun. The first pair of jets overflew us and we turned into a valley very low down indeed. Just as we did so, to get into a position where the jets couldn't follow, I heard a pretty nasty burst of cannon fire.

'We landed in a bowl, had a look round and found a cannon shell had penetrated the spar of one of the main rotor blades. It had held together however, and we were pretty grateful to the manufacturers.'

In the *Sir Galahad* rescue operation Lt John Miller and PO Aircrewman Alan Ashdown in 'Victor Zulu' were off-loading Rapier AA weapons from the ship and were about 200 yards towards the shore when they saw the Argentinian attack go in. They hovered out of sight behind some high ground for a few minutes then moved in to lift survivors from the foredeck and fly them ashore four or five at a time. They were flying in smoke for most of the time, hovering at about 20ft with ammunition exploding on the ship. Both men were Mentioned in Despatches.

Above: CPO 'Alf' Tupper. *RN*

Right: Most of the Navy's Sea Kings armed themselves with general purpose machine guns mounted in the rear door. This picture was in fact taken in a No 819 Squadron aircraft during exercises over the Otterburn ranges in Northumberland.
Leading Airman (Phot) Chris North/RN

Altogether 21 decorations were won by members of No 846 Squadron including an MBE awarded to the engineering officer, Lt S. J. Branch-Evans RN, and a posthumous DSM to Cpl Michael Love, Royal Marines, the aircrewman who died in the tragic accident to 'Victor Tango' on 19 May.

The cause of this crash in which 21 died, 18 of them members of the Special Air Service Regiment, has not been publicly disclosed although the possibility of the aircraft being struck by an albatross (which could have weighed up to 17lbs) at a critical point in the flight was advanced at one stage. The remains of a large bird were seen amongst the wreckage flostsam. Nine aboard, including the two pilots, survived 'with difficulty', it was officially recorded. The accident happened during a transfer between HMS *Hermes* and *Intrepid.*

No 846 Squadron's other loss, that of ZA311, involved a single-pilot night Vertrep from HMS *Hermes* on 23 April 1982 while the Fleet was still on its way south from Ascension. The aircrewman, PO K. S. ('Doc') Casey died, the pilot was rescued.

Some mystery understandably continued to surround the deliberate burning of ZA290 ('Victor Charlie') on Chilean soil on 20 May, but it became generally accepted that the aircraft had been involved in placing a clandestine observation party on enemy territory, had encountered weather preventing its return to its mother ship, and that the captain and crew decided on their course of action to protect the mission's overall integrity.

The two pilots, Lt Alan Bennett RN and Lt Richard Hutchings RM who with their unnamed crewman stayed in hiding for many days, were both awarded the DSC for their work on night missions with No 846 Squadron. No specific mention was made in either officer's decoration citation to the Chilean episode.

On the credit side No 846 Squadron 'gained' an aircraft, after the pilot of 'Victor Sierra' had to plump down hard and fast on some Falklands bogland when coming under unexpected fire and wrote off most of the tail rotor assembly in the process. Some time earlier a Mk 2 of No 825 Squadron (XV696, side number 68), had met a sad though temporary fate when one of its main undercarriage wheels penetrated the crust of a typical stretch of Falklands peat and toppled over with rotors turning. This aircraft was cannibalised a little at a time and in a remarkable piece of field engineering the maintainers of No 846 Squadron lifted and fitted its entire tail rotor pylon assembly on to 'Victor Sierra', in the open, without a crane, but with the judicious use of packing cases and some residual knowledge of how the Pyramids were built. 'Victor Sierra', in a rather strange colour combination which would defy the most assiduous of model makers, flew in time to give No 846 Squadron an 11-aircraft strength for the final advance to Port Stanley, every one of its aeroplanes needed urgently in

Left: 'Victor Sierra' stripped and ready for rebuild. *No 846 NAS/RN*

view of the loss of all but one of the RAF Chinooks in the *Atlantic Conveyor* attack. The remains of No 825 Squadron's XV696 were brought back and after an extensive rebuild at Culdrose the airframe bearing this number is flying again.

Lt Branch-Evans (the engineering officer of No 846 Squadron) came back from the Falklands justifiably proud of his team which had achieved an average 85% overall availability, moving up to 100% for the final advance on to Stanley.

Below: The tail pylon from No 825 Squadron's '68' being brought into line — a ton or so of it. *No 846 NAS/RN*

Bottom: The tail pylon being lifted into position without benefit of cranes or ladders, but by the skilful combination of the use of packing cases and 'Muscles, Maintainers Mk 1'. *No 846 NAS/RN*

Top: 'Victor Sierra' flying again after the rebuild in Port William. This aircraft later played a major part in the final 'Yomp', most of the much-needed Chinooks having been destroyed. *No 846 NAS/RN*

Above and right: A No 846 Squadron Mk 4 being refuelled at Teal Inlet using rubber air portable fuel containers. *No 846 NAS/RN*

Left: A Mk 2 of 825 Squadron landing on *Canberra's* hastily organised helicopter spot. *RN*

Below left: The No 825 Squadron crews first lived in tents 'begged, borrowed or stolen' from other arms. The maintainers learned to live and work in conditions vastly different from heated hangars at Culdrose and even from ships' hangars. *RN*

Below: They began to creep into more solid buildings and developed self-supporting culinary arts.

Squadron was heading towards the South Atlantic embarked in *Queen Elizabeth II* and *Atlantic Causeway* with a rearguard following on board the RFA *Engadine*.

A high proportion of the aircraft and personnel inevitably came from No 706 Squadron which Lt-Cdr Clark was commanding at the time of receipt of his unexpected orders but stiffenings of both came from Nos 814, 819 and 824 Squadrons. The Mk 2 Sea Kings acquired were: XZ580, (side number 72); XV659 (84), XV663 (95), XV648 (97), XV700 (64), XV696 (68), XV656 (03), XV677 (91), XV654 (85) and XV714 (86). All ASW gear was stripped out of the aircraft giving them a troop carrying capacity of between 16 and 24 according to range, and alternative stretcher accommodation in the casualty evacuation role. Radios giving direct links to ground troop frequencies were fitted.

On the voyage over the aircraft were coated with a corrosion proof substance like that used for the internal sealing of motor car bodies, giving them a sort of greenish look, somewhat akin to that of the Commando Mk 4s DTD555 Olive Drab, but not quite the same, and apparently unreproduceable by fastidious model makers and their miniature paint support industry. It was washed off again on the way back, restoring the aeroplanes to their original, curiously labelled RAF blue-grey, finish. (In common with all other naval aircraft taking part in the conflict the whites of roundels were painted out either in red or blue or a bit of each; white side or pennant numbers were overpainted in black, and any rotor pylon base identification letters were obliterated.)

During the conflict No 825 Squadron amassed 1,756 flying hours, 394 sorties and 1,051 deck landings. During the month of June pilots averaged

Left: Sea Kings were sometimes reluctant to start in these conditions but almost always did eventually.

Below: Again — the sort of conditions which helicopters and their air and ground crews dislike intensely.

Bottom: 'Wellies', and some 'acquired' military clothing, helped, and skills were developed over such matters as the barbecuing of Falkland mutton.

Lt-Cdr Clark's own recollections are that at the time it seemed to be a fairly routine rescue operation, considerably less complicated than those like the *Lovat* and *Merc Enterprise* jobs in the southwest of England in which he and CPO Jackson had been involved many years earlier. He was able to maintain a satisfactory 20ft hover over the stern of the ship by using the lettering *Sir Galahad* on the starboard quarter as a visual reference even through the billows of smoke. After lifting those who could put themselves into the rescue strop and ferrying them ashore, the crew adopted the expedient of helping the liferafts still loaded with badly burned Welsh Guardsmen by blowing them in the right direction on the periphery of the helicopter downwash.

Three other No 825 Squadron Sea Kings took part in the *Sir Galahad* rescue together with John Miller's Mk 4 from No 846 Squadron and a Commando Squadron Wessex. Lt Phil Sheldon and Lt John Boughton of No 825 Squadron were awarded the Queen's Gallantry Medal for their part as aircraft captains. Apart from the decorations mentioned so far another 11 Culdrose-based personnel, most of them associated with the Falklands Sea King operations, received awards. For once due recognition was paid to the hours of work and devotion to duty put in by many who stayed behind and drove themselves to the limit to provide the essential back-up services. Purveyors of suitable refreshment around the station recall many grey faces with sunken eyes appearing across their bars for very brief periods during the spring and early summer months of 1982.

Although much of the information relating to it is classified it is fairly widely known that the Sea Kings played an important part in various aspects of the 'electronic war' in the Falklands and details of the fitting of Electronic Support Measures (ESM) equipment to them were reported publicly in late 1982. Their use as distributors of Chaff — known in World War 2 as Window — to confuse enemy radar, and occasionally to act as decoys to divert incoming Exocets was also widely reported.

Consideration is believed to have been given at one stage to equipping some of them with anti-surface vessel missiles using improvised launching racks but while this was obviously feasible it was not proceeded with. Most of the Nos 846 and 825 Squadron aircraft carried GPMGs on cargo door mountings but there is no record of them having been fired in anger. 'We just waved them around to frighten the opposition — didn't want to actually *hurt* anyone' was the comment of one very senior aircrewman.

No 202 Squadron RAF detached one of its Mk 3 Sea Kings from its 'C' Flight at Coltishall at an early stage to assist in the build-up operation and this aircraft was flown out to Ascension in a former RAF Belfast transport, one of the fleet now operated by Heavy Lift Cargo Airlines of Stansted Airport. This method of delivery, involving the removal of the main rotor head and gearbox, the tail rotor pylon and the undercarriage sponsons, had been proved earlier in the transport of a Sea King to India, and it went without hitch.

The first No 202 Squadron aircraft, still in its yellow rescue livery, was used for stores and personnel transfer work at Ascension before being moved south and joined by others from the same unit to form a semi-permanent detachment in the Falklands garrison for SAR and general work. The No 202 Squadron detachment aircraft are now painted grey with their 'RESCUE' lettering still in black and a muted form of the Mallard crest on the nose. They have been equipped with additional navigation equipment, the details of which are classified. Air and ground crews from all four flights of the Squadron do regular four-month tours of duty in the South Atlantic and generally welcome them since the RAF's SAR world tends to be a somewhat static one in service terms. The SAR commitment at Coltishall has been taken over by Wessex aircraft, this being the one No 202 Squadron location least in need of long-range helicopters.

Left: Lt Phil Sheldon and Lt John Boughton of No 825 Squadron. Both were awarded the Queen's Gallantry Medal for their parts in the *Sir Galahad* rescue. *RN*

This picture: An HAR3 of No 202 Squadron RAF transferring stores off Ascension during the Falklands build-up.
Paul Haley, Soldier Magazine

Above and above right: The first RAF Sea King was flown out to Ascension in a Belfast freighter of Heavy Lift Cargo Airlines. These two pictures show the system of loading although the first is a RN Mk 5 and the second an Indian Navy aircraft. *RN/David L. Lipson*

Right: The first Mk 2s of No 824 Squadron as converted to the Airborne Early Warning role with radomes lowered. *Westland*

An important outcome of the Falklands conflict was the hasty conversion of two Sea King Mk 2s of No 824 NAS into Airborne Early Warning aircraft. The lack of this type of cover, specifically offering detection of the Exocet-carrying Argentinian Super Etendards, became clear at an early stage. A combined effort involving Westlands, Thorne EMI and the RN produced in 8½ weeks two Sea Kings capable of doing the job. Many within the last-named organisation wish someone had thought of the idea a little sooner. The two AEW Sea Kings, XV650 and XV704 (the first being one of the earliest Mk 1s to begin its service in the Navy), now comprise 'D' Flight of No 824 Squadron and were taken to the Falklands along with the Mk 5s of No 814 Squadron in HMS *Illustrious* soon after hostilities ended. They carry Thorne EMI Searchwater radar sets similar to those fitted to the RAF's Nimrod Mk 2 AEW aircraft. They

Left: Radomes raised for take-off or landing. The 1983 Defence White Paper announced the provision of 11 of these aircraft.

Below left: Lt-Cdr Mike Brougham, Air Engineering Officer of No 825 Squadron, who was awarded the MBE for 'sound direction, engineering and organisational skills'. *RN*

Below: CPO John Williams, awarded the British Empire Medal as senior rating in charge of the engine repair shop at Culdrose. Learning of the exceptional priority for Sea King engines he abandoned his Easter leave and recalled his men. His section turned out as many repaired engines in two months as they would normally have done in six. *RN*

What Next?

Above: A Culdrose Sea King launching a Sting Ray torpedo on trials. *RN*

At the time of writing in the spring of 1984 many in the RN were reiterating the suggestion made in the introduction that the basic Westland Sea King airframe would still be in srvice in the 21st century, albeit with different things inside it and other things 'hung on it'. The latter ability has historically been a requirement of most aircraft operated by the RN. The Sea King's ability to cope with such matters had by then been abundantly proven, especially during the Falklands war, concluding with the rapid conversions of Mk 2s into the AEW aircraft described in the last chapter.

A Sea King replacement design, the Westland-Agusta (Italy) EH101 was in an advanced embryo stage in 1984 but with its basic features clearly established and identified. In America the Sikorsky Seahawk was already in full scale production as a replacement for the USNs latest H-3s (their Sea Kings) with other Hawk variants adopted by the US Army and the USAF.

For at least another five years however, even with the revelations about 26,000ton Soviet 'catamaran' submarines, the future of RN helicopter anti-submarine operations seemed to lie with even more refinements to the Sea King, including the adoption of retrofit composite main and tail rotor blades. In the RAF's SAR world several improvements were in hand including the fitting of reserve winches referred to earlier. Others included the development of better communications between winchmen on the bottom end of 200ft or more of wire and the aircraft above them, by the adoption of new bone-dome helmets incorporating short-range VHF radio sets. The idea of going back to the earlier system of wiring-in a telephone cable was looked at but discarded — the very first two-man crew RN rescue Dragonflies were fitted with such a system but it seldom worked because of the effect of water upon the circuit connections.

The RAF was also hoping to introduce the Selcal (selective calling) system into its radio communications pack to reduce the crew fatigue induced by having to listen out for four or five different voices or callsigns at once, and in particular having to endure the constant eardrum-assaulting 'mush' and morse cacophony on the long-range HF band. Selcal is a well-proved system used for many years in commercial and service transport aircraft in which an aircrew can almost literally be 'rung up' by a caller and can switch to an appropriate frequency when a bell rings or a light flashes.

The use of Nightsun, the high intensity lighting system used extensively by Army Air Corps helicopters particularly in Northern Ireland and by Bristow in its rescue helicopters operating over the North Sea oil rigs, was also considered by the RAF SAR Wing for its Sea Kings but rejected on at least two counts, firstly that two aircraft are normally needed to use it effectively — one to light up the scene, another to carry out the rescue — and secondly because high intensity light is inevitably accompanied by high intensity heat, and this can be complicating, especially if anything inflammable is immediately present. Considerable improvements in the whole night vision field had already been achieved both in the RAF and in the RN by the use of image-intensification goggles by aircrews. A number of very difficult night rescue operations had also proved that the existing Sea King lighting system was usually adequate.

In the FAA a number of classified developments had come into service by 1984, in hand for the Mk 5 Sea Kings, it being known publicly that one included an improved form of LAPADS display for passive sonar operations which would make life easier for the hard worked 'back-end' crews.

In the field of weaponry the Sting Ray torpedo was already coming into service in 1983 and being carried by the Royal Navy's Mk 5 Sea Kings. It was due to go on in service until the 1990s and would be part of the equipment of the EH101s and possibly beyond. Its manufacturer, Marconi Space & Defence System, has described it as not a torpedo in the traditional sense of the word but more 'an intelligent underwater weapon'. Its tactical performance, Marconi sales literature says, depends on a computer-based guidance system, and it claims that it is the first underwater weapon to use a programmable digital computer to control its behaviour. All this, and more, adds to the prospect of Sting Ray-loaded Sea Kings going on flying with the RN into that 21st century. The published description of Sting Ray's performance says that when it enters the sea a salt water propulsion battery is activated. The weapon then searches for the target, using an electronically steered multi-beam sonar, and having acquired the target homes in on it and stays locked-on despite enemy countermeasures or evasive manoeuvres. Its heart is a fast micro-miniature computer which controls the whole operation, enabling it to distinguish targets from counter-measures. The computer automatically selects search patterns appropriate to water conditions, computes the intercept course, receives information on the target, returns and analyses it to decide on the measures to be adopted in the face of alterations by the enemy in course, speed or depth. It is the first underwater weapon to use a programmable digital computer to control its behaviour and an important feature is its ability to operate quietly in both deep and shallow water. (The Mk 44 torpedo, long the main armament of ASW Sea Kings, has been regarded as obsolete for some years in terms of reaching the known operating depths of Soviet submarines and the Mk 46 (Mod 2) which was purchased from the United States in the 1970s as an interim weapon has limitations in shallow water and in countermeasures performance.)

The capability of the Sea King to carry anti-surface weapons had already been abundantly proved by 1983 and it will be clearly adaptable to almost anything new

Left: Sea Kings could probably go on flying for days with in-flight refuelling; the crews cannot. A Mk 5 of No 810 Squadron off *Engadine's* deck. *RN*

which weapon manufacturers may evolve over the next decade or more.

It was in the field of 'ergonomics', particularly related to the exacting tasks of its Observer officers and sonar operator aircrewmen in the back of the aircraft that the RN most wanted to see improvements and active work on the problems was going on at Westland and elsewhere in 1984. When the Sea King first came into service it was regarded as a luxury vehicle compared with the Wessex or Whirlwind but the stresses, partly due to noise and vibration, on back seat crews had been assessed as high. The Observer and Sonar Operator are also not only working in confined quarters but in semi-darkness as well in order to view various cathode ray screens and other instruments. They feel they deserve and need the best possible comfort that can be afforded to them on sheer grounds of efficiency. (There is an intriguing theory in the FAA that helicopter Observers always produce male children — one which might earn an earnest researcher a lucrative grant some day.) The case for greater comfort was well proved during the Falklands war when crew fatigue certainly became a limiting factor, keeping sortie lengths down to the long-established four to five hours, except in dire emergencies, even if in-flight refuelling could have kept the aircraft flying almost indefinitely.

Westland had been working on composite blade (and other component) construction for more than 15 years by 1983, and had set aside 30,000sq ft of its Yeovil factory for the projects, due to be expanded to 120,000sq ft by 1984. As well as evolving a composite blade design for the EH101 project and for later versions of the Lynx the company had reached an advanced flight test stage for retrofit Sea King blades in 1983 with a test aircraft (the faithful XV642) flying a complete tail rotor and one composite main rotor blade. The principal advantage claimed for the composite blade is longevity but in the Royal and other navies resistance to accidental damage could be a bonus. Spanners and other heavy and blunt instruments can fall on helicopter blades in heavy weather in the hangars of the best conducted ships. So far as the Sea King retrofit composite blades are concerned weight is not a factor, the whole idea is to make replacements exactly compatible with the metal equivalents in terms of size, profile, weight and 'cuff' fitting on to the rotor head.

A formal contract between Britain and Italy for the EH101 project was signed in 1984 with 1985 the planned first flight date and commercial deliveries scheduled for 1987-8. The MoD has given the project a firm blessing as a Sea King replacement. The general concept is for a three-engined aircraft, slightly smaller in overall dimensions than the Sea King but with more manoeuvrability, power reserve and disposable load capacity enabling it to operate from smaller ships, particularly the next generation of frigates. Its main armament in the ASW role is almost certain to be the Sting Ray torpedo and its primary hunting equipment Ferranti Blue Kestrel search radar. The GE T700-401 has been selected as the power plant.

On the other side of the Atlantic the most important immediate development by 1983 had been the proving

Below: Artist's impression of what the EH101 *may* look like. The planned positioning of the radome under the nose instead of on top of the fuselage is of interest. *Westland*

and large scale production of the Hawk series of helicopters by Sikorsky. As an aftermath of the Vietnam war American manufacturers had been invited to compete for the design of a new medium size troop carrying helicopter for the US Army. Sikorsky won, in 1976, what was termed the UTTAS (Utility Tactical Transport Aircraft System) competition against Boeing Vertol. The Sikorsky design, S-70 in company designation, H-60 in United States forces language, first entered service with the Army as the Black Hawk, or UH-60A. The basic design has followed Igor Sikorsky's 'penny farthing' single main and anti-torque tail rotor concept but with high-lift aerofoil section mainblades. The four-bladed tail rotor is of epoxy-graphite composite construction and the power comes from a pair of General Electric T-700 turboshafts. The Seahawks, second in the family and built under an initial USN requirement for 204 aircraft, will be operated from frigates, destroyers and cruisers and are in a broad sense the replacement for the American H-3s (Sea Kings). In obtaining this contract Sikorsky had won another competition, this time called 'LAMPS III' (Light Airborne Multi-Purpose System Mk III). The US Navy designation of the Seahawk is SH-60B, or S-70L in company terms. One of its special features is the RAST (recovery, assist, secure and traversing) equipment developed by DAF/Indal of Canada from its earlier Beartrap design which is used by Canadian Sikorsky-built SH-3D Sea Kings. Main and tail rotor deicing equipment is also provided. The third of the S-70 family is thc HH-60D Night Hawk adopted by the USAF as a combat rescue helicopter.

Longer term development in the Sikorsky stable is now concentrated on the ABC (Advancing Blade Concept) aircraft, breaking away at last from anti-torque tail rotor configuration and using coaxial contra-rotating main rotors plus auxiliary thrust jet or ducted fan engines and some fixed lifting surface.

Among the most important developments going on at Stratford, Connecticut of especial interest to the RN with its identified ergonomics problem, were revolutionary pilot control systems, including a 'side arm controller' which perhaps in lay terms could be related to the armchair control box of a television set.

Although Sikorsky was obviously seeking overseas markets for its Hawks and hoping for co-production or licence manufacturing agreements in 1983 this aircraft was *not* regarded in Britain as even an interim replacement for the Sea King even if the nation had the money to buy it off the shelf. Quite apart from the advanced state of the EH101 project involving two, possibly three, European countries, the RN had only a professional/curiosity interest in the Seahawk. A special factor remained the widening difference between the Royal and the US Navies in their tactical handling of, and crewing of, ASW hunter-killer helicopters. The latter service still adhered to the principle of pilots at the front end of the aeroplane being 'in charge' rather than the specialist-trained Observer officers and Sonar Operator aircrewmen at the back end which the RN believes to be the right arrangement and which it believes it has proved in hundreds of exercises and one war.

Apart from all its other claims to fame, therefore, the Westland Sea King might go down in aeronautical history as the last in line of the long standing Westland-Sikorsky 'arrangement' which did, when all is said and done, provide for the British nation its first generations of effective helicopters, which have taken few lives, have saved many, and which have helped keep potential enemies at bay.

Right: The EH101 will be produced by EH Industries Ltd, a company controlled jointly by Westland Helicopters in the UK and Agusta, the Italian manufacturer. *Westland*

Appendices

1 Westland Sea King Specifications

Type: Twin engine, single main rotor helicopter
Design Maximum Take-Off and Landing Weight: 9,524kg (21,000lb)
Power Plant: Two Rolls-Royce Gnome H1400-1 engines (standard for temperate zones); two Rolls-Royce Gnome H1400-1T engines (standard for High Ambient temperature zones)
Performance (HAS Mk 5): 208km/hr (130mph) max cruising speed at sea level; 1.9m/sec (390ft/min) max vertical rate of climb; 1,507km (937 miles) max ferry range
Main Rotor Diameter: 18.90m (62ft 0in)
Tail Rotor Diameter: 3.15m (10ft 4in)
Overall Length (rotors turning): 22.15m (72ft 8in)
Overall Height (rotors spread and stationary): 4.97m (16ft 4in)
Overall Height (rotors turning): 5.13m (16ft 10in)
Cabin Length: 7.6m (24ft 11in)
Cabin Width (maximum): 2.0m (6ft 6in)
Cabin Height (centre line of aircraft: 1.9m (6ft 3.5in)
Height to Main Cargo Door Sill: 1.14m (3ft 9in)
Personnel Door Size — Port: 0.91m × 1.67m (3ft 0in × 5ft 6in)
Main Cargo Door Size — Starboard: 1.72m × 1.52m (5ft 8in × 5ft 0in)
Main Rotor Blade Chord: 0.46m (18.25in)
Tail Rotor Blade Chord: 0.186m (7.34in)
Main Rotor Blade Thickness (% Chord): 12%
Tail Rotor Blade Thickness (% Chord): 12%
Track of Main Wheels: 3.96m (13ft 0in)

2 Role Equipment

1 ANTI-SUBMARINE WARFARE (ASW)
Detection Systems
(a) Dipping sonar:
  Plessy 195
  Bendix AN/AQS13B
  Bendix AN/AQS18
(b) Magnetic anomaly detector (MAD):
  Texas Instruments AN/ASQ81
(c) Lightweight acoustic processing and display systems (LAPADS)
  Sonobuoy racking

2 SEARCH AND RESCUE
(a) 18 seated survivors:
  18 seats installation
  Rescue winch and spotlight
  Waterproof floor (short/long)
(b) 11 seated and 3 stretcher survivors:
  11 seats installation
  3 stretcher installation (starboard)
  Rescue winch and spotlight
  Waterproof floor (short/long)
  Water boiler
  Liferafts (2)

3 LONG RANGE PATROL, RECONNAISSANCE AND OFF-SHORE SUPPORT
  Auxiliary fuel tank
  3 seats installation
  VIPA 1: camera pod installation

4 CASUALTY EVACUATION
  10 seated and 6 stretcher survivors:
  10 seats installation
  6 stretcher installation (3 port, 3 starboard)
  Rescue winch and spotlight
  Waterproof floor (short/long)
  Water boiler

5 LOGISTIC SUPPORT
(a) External freight:
  External freight sling (6,000lb capacity)
  External freight sling (8,000lb capacity)
(b) Troop Transport:
  23 seat installation
  Monorail for paratroops

6 ANTI-SURFACE VESSEL (ASV)
  AM39 Exocet missile installation (fixed and removable)

7 MISCELLANEOUS EQUIPMENT
  Air conditioning BGL pack and piping
  Removable flotation gear
  Sand filter
  FOD — without anti-icing
  FOD — with anti-icing
  Anti-icing system for FOD (fixed)
  Anti-icing fluid

8 ARMAMENT

(a) ASW Role:
- Torpedo/depth charge carriers
- Mk 46 torpedo
- Marine markers
- Smoke/flame floats
- Sonobuoys Type A
- Type F

(b) Troop Transport:
- 7.62mm GPMG pintle mounted
- Ammunition boxes and stowage
- Ammunition 800 rounds
- Parachuting monorail

(c) ASV Role:
- Missile launcher per station
- Exocet missiles

3 Typical Role Configurations

Casualty evacuation

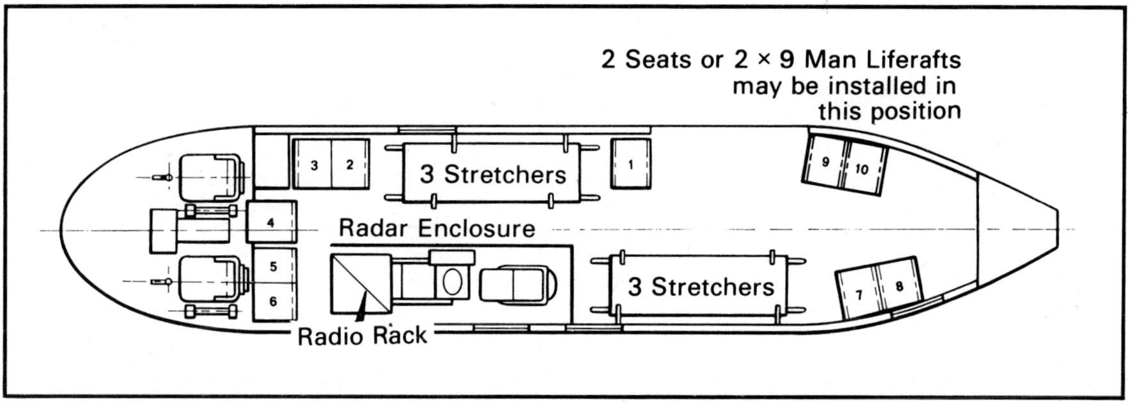

Search and rescue — 18 seats

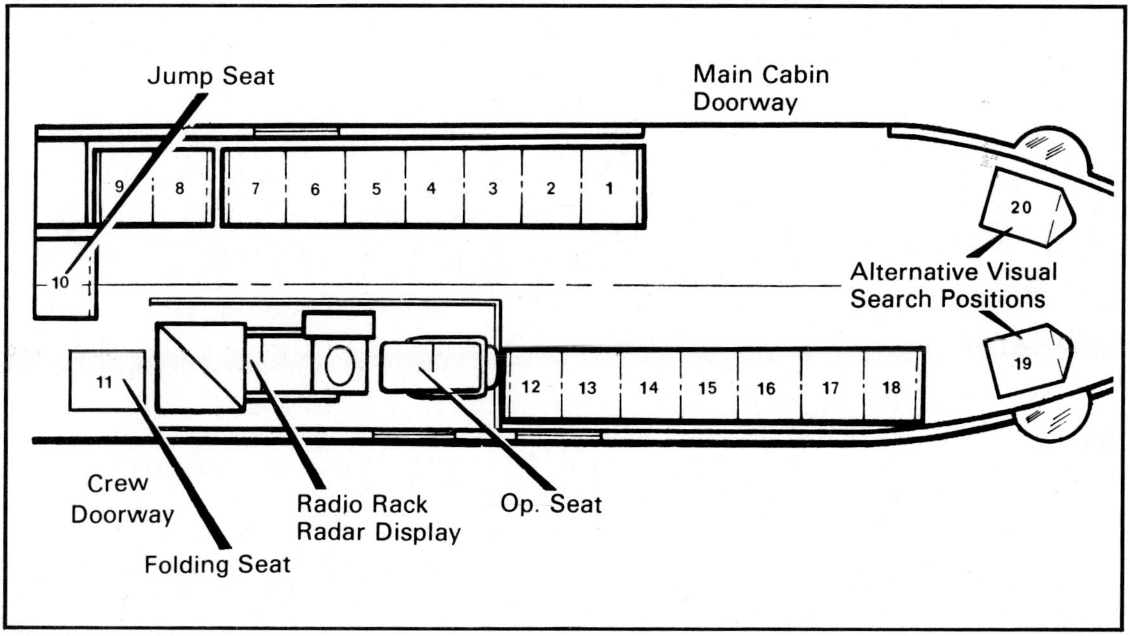

Search and rescue — 11 seats and 3 stretchers

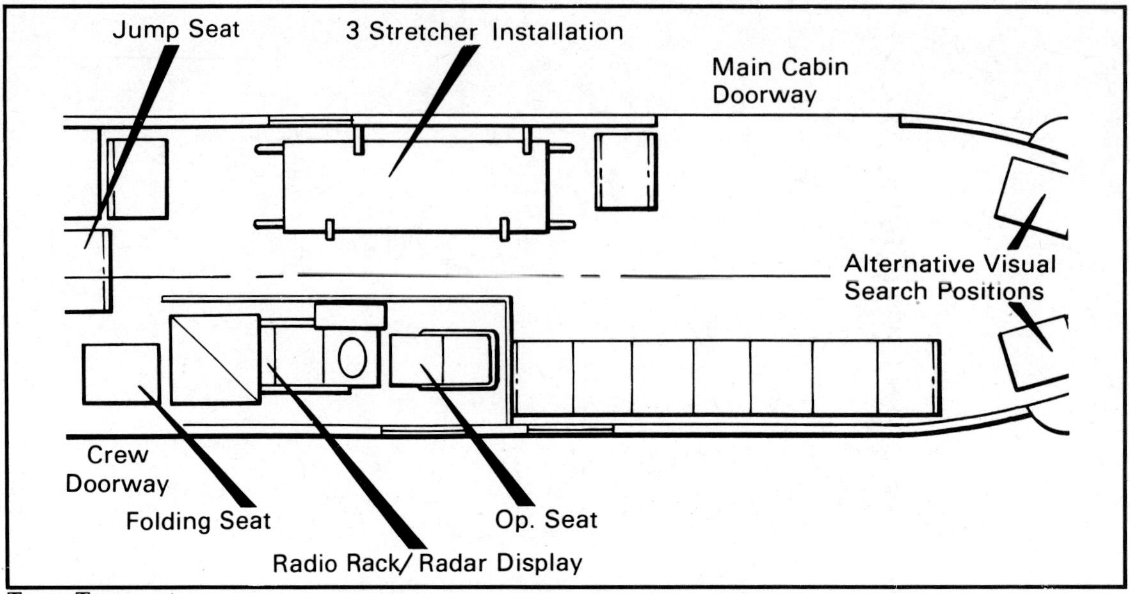

Troop Transport

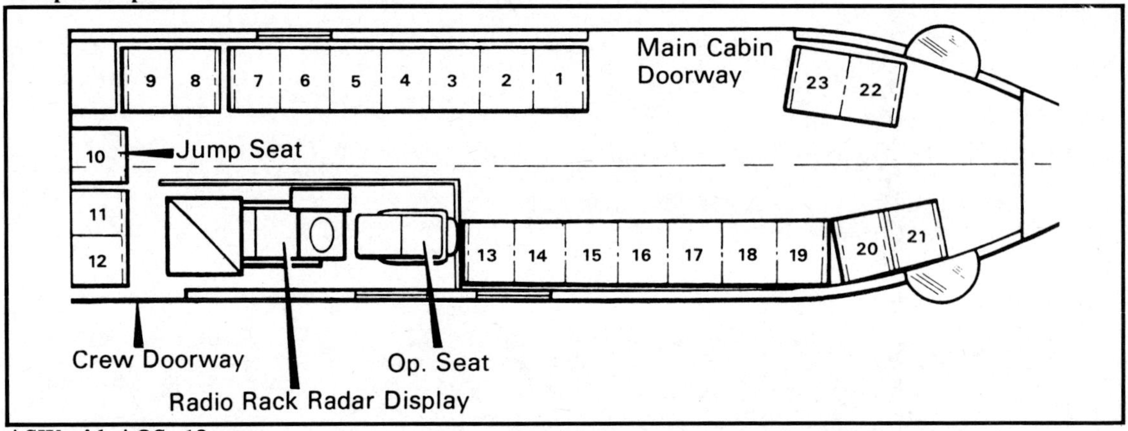

ASW with AQS–18 sonar

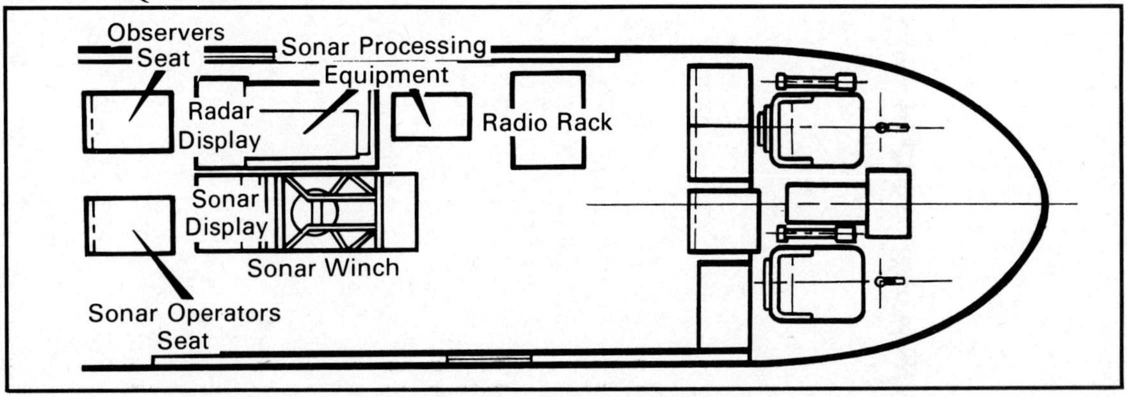

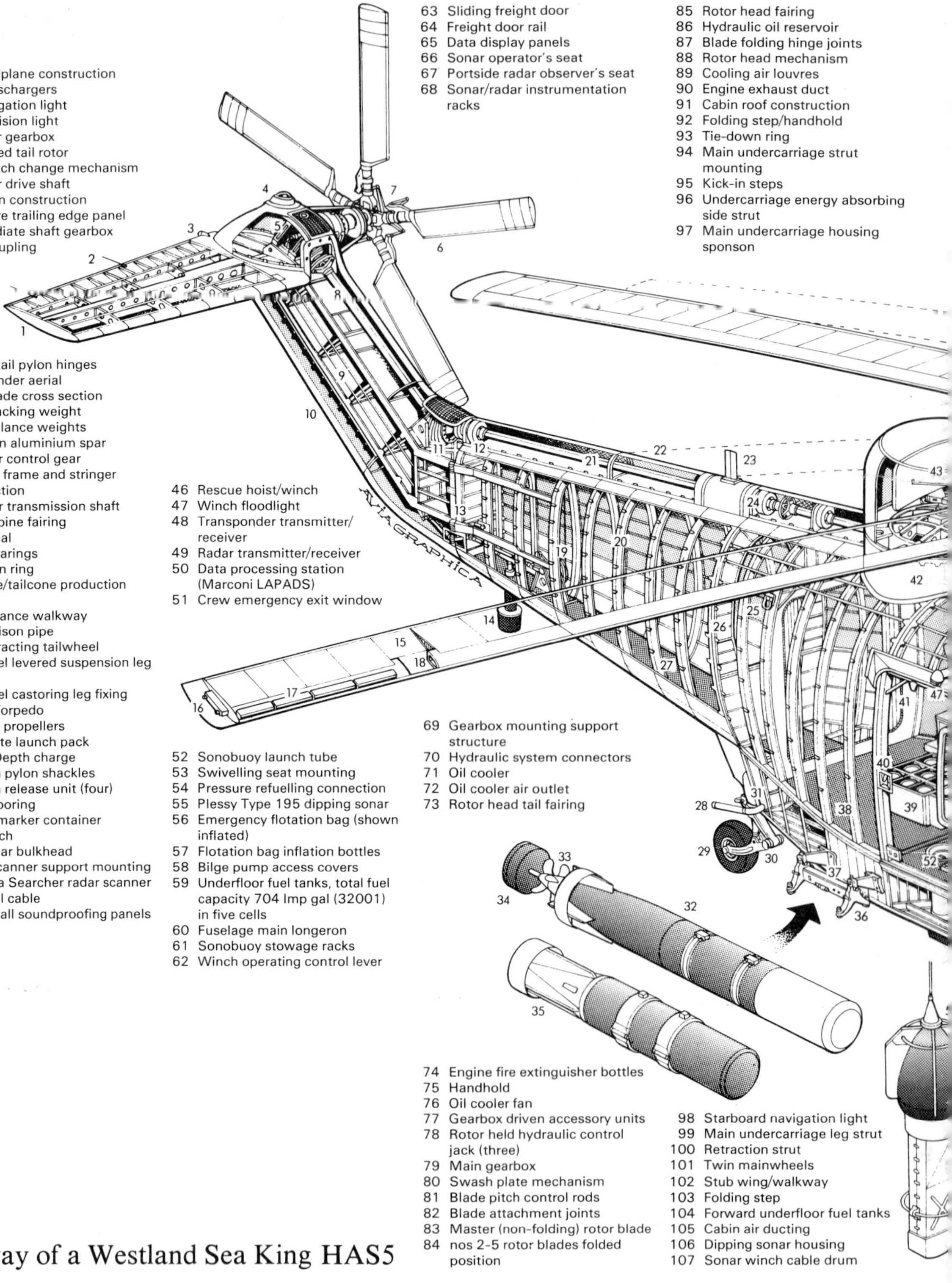

Cutaway of a Westland Sea King HAS5

1 Fixed tailplane construction
2 Static dischargers
3 Tail navigation light
4 Anti-collision light
5 Tail rotor gearbox
6 Six-bladed tail rotor
7 Blade pitch change mechanism
8 Tail rotor drive shaft
9 Tail pylon construction
10 Glassfibre trailing edge panel
11 Intermediate shaft gearbox
12 Shaft coupling
13 Folding tail pylon hinges
14 Transponder aerial
15 Rotor blade cross section
16 Blade tracking weight
17 Blade balance weights
18 D-section aluminium spar
19 Tail rotor control gear
20 Tailcone frame and stringer construction
21 Tail rotor transmission shaft
22 Dorsal spine fairing
23 UHF aerial
24 Shaft bearings
25 Tie-down ring
26 Fuselage/tailcone production joint
27 Maintenance walkway
28 Fuel jettison pipe
29 Non-retracting tailwheel
30 Tailwheel levered suspension leg strut
31 Tailwheel castoring leg fixing
32 Mk 46 Torpedo
33 Torpedo propellers
34 Parachute launch pack
35 Mk 11 Depth charge
36 Weapon pylon shackles
37 Weapon release unit (four)
38 Cabin flooring
39 Smoke marker container
40 Door latch
41 Cabin rear bulkhead
42 Radar scanner support mounting
43 MEL Sea Searcher radar scanner
44 HF aerial cable
45 Cabin wall soundproofing panels
46 Rescue hoist/winch
47 Winch floodlight
48 Transponder transmitter/receiver
49 Radar transmitter/receiver
50 Data processing station (Marconi LAPADS)
51 Crew emergency exit window
52 Sonobuoy launch tube
53 Swivelling seat mounting
54 Pressure refuelling connection
55 Plessy Type 195 dipping sonar
56 Emergency flotation bag (shown inflated)
57 Flotation bag inflation bottles
58 Bilge pump access covers
59 Underfloor fuel tanks, total fuel capacity 704 Imp gal (32001) in five cells
60 Fuselage main longeron
61 Sonobuoy stowage racks
62 Winch operating control lever
63 Sliding freight door
64 Freight door rail
65 Data display panels
66 Sonar operator's seat
67 Portside radar observer's seat
68 Sonar/radar instrumentation racks
69 Gearbox mounting support structure
70 Hydraulic system connectors
71 Oil cooler
72 Oil cooler air outlet
73 Rotor head tail fairing
74 Engine fire extinguisher bottles
75 Handhold
76 Oil cooler fan
77 Gearbox driven accessory units
78 Rotor held hydraulic control jack (three)
79 Main gearbox
80 Swash plate mechanism
81 Blade pitch control rods
82 Blade attachment joints
83 Master (non-folding) rotor blade
84 nos 2-5 rotor blades folded position
85 Rotor head fairing
86 Hydraulic oil reservoir
87 Blade folding hinge joints
88 Rotor head mechanism
89 Cooling air louvres
90 Engine exhaust duct
91 Cabin roof construction
92 Folding step/handhold
93 Tie-down ring
94 Main undercarriage strut mounting
95 Kick-in steps
96 Undercarriage energy absorbing side strut
97 Main undercarriage housing sponson
98 Starboard navigation light
99 Main undercarriage leg strut
100 Retraction strut
101 Twin mainwheels
102 Stub wing/walkway
103 Folding step
104 Forward underfloor fuel tanks
105 Cabin air ducting
106 Dipping sonar housing
107 Sonar winch cable drum